An Inconvenient Text

Is a Green Reading of the Bible Possible?

Norman Habel

ATF Press
Adelaide

National Library of Australia Cataloguing-in-Publication entry

Author: Habel, Norman C.

Title: An inconvenient text : is a green reading of the Bible possible
                / Norman Habel.

ISBN: 9781921511561 (pbk.)

Subjects: Bible--Criticism, interpretation, etc.
                Environmental degradation--Religious aspects--Christianity.
                Environmental protection--Religious aspects--Christianity.
                Environmental responsibility--Religious aspects.
                Environmentalism--Religious aspects--Christianity.
                Human ecology--Religious aspects.

Dewey Number: 261.88

Published by ATF Press

An imprint of the Australasian Theological Forum Ltd
PO BOX 504 Hindmarsh
SA 5007
ABN 90 116 359 963
www.atfpress.com

Cover design by Astrid Sengkey
Original artwork by Simeon Nasilowski

Unless otherwise specified all Bible translations will be from the New Revised Standard Version (NRSV)

In memory of
Alfred von Rohr Sauer
my mentor and second father
who would have been 100
as I write
my preface
6 December 2008
and his wife
Ellie Sauer
my second mother

Preface

Norman Habel has written a book that has been needed for some time. Aptly entitled *An Inconvenient Text*, it is a rigorous analysis of the ecological ambivalence of Scripture. Eschewing cosmetic cover-ups, he insists on an honest look at the Bible in light of the twenty-first century worldview of where humanity fits on planet Earth. From this perspective, favorite texts such as those concerning the mandate to dominate, the mighty acts of God, and the right to the promised land come in for radically new interpretations.

The revolutionary and unique task Habel sets himself is a hard-headed reading from a postmodern, scientific, ecological worldview. This is not a matter of finding 'green' passages in the Bible, or even of rescuing questionable—which he calls 'grey'—ones. Rather, it is a move away from the modern individualistic anthropocentric paradigm at the heart of our insatiable consumer culture that has fueled the twin crises of climate change and economic collapse. Taking a different perspective—the view of the interrelationship and interdependence of all life-forms, including human beings—Habel has produced a wonderfully readable, passionate, and incisive book that is a major contribution to the religion and ecology conversation.

That conversation has become considerably more sophisticated over the last forty years, with Professor Habel as one of the principal participants. What began as an attempt to 'save the Bible' through reading problematic texts in terms of what they 'could' mean or 'did' mean, and to identify texts that showed Jesus' fondness for natural settings (as well as fig trees and hens), has resulted in a realisation that the religions of the world can contribute to the destruction, or to the flourishing, of our planet.

Religions are major players in forming people's most basic assumptions about who we are in the scheme of things, and about what we should be doing. As counter-cultural worldviews, they offer one of the few critiques of the reigning individualistic consumer sensibility that is destroying our planet. They can also suggest more just and sustainable alternatives. It is difficult to over-emphasise the seriousness of the climatic and financial crises that are calling into question our mismanagement of the earth. The task of religious scholars is no longer to try to redeem their own traditions as 'green' in some way or another; rather, the issue is their mandate to contribute to a just and sustainable worldview for planetary flourishing.

Norman Habel's book is about this task. He takes his hermeneutical stance from within the twenty-first century ecological worldview and asks whether the Bible can be partner in our planetary agenda. As he writes, 'A greening of biblical studies means standing in a very different place when we read. We stand with Earth and read for Earth and the Earth community.'

In this important and lively book, Habel grounds his insightful comments in a particular context—stories from his own Australia—that gives 'voice' to Earth—not only in general but in particular. It is rare to find a book that is at the same time a major contribution to the most important conversation of our time—and delightful read.

An Inconvenient Text is such a book.

Sallie McFague
Vancouver School of Theology, Canada
November 2008

Foreword

Ecological problems such as climate change require a multidisciplinary approach in which every one of us is called upon to play a role. Despite the earlier criticisms by Lynn White Jr and others regarding the complicity of Christianity in environmental destruction, it has now become clear that the role of religion will be critical in addressing such destruction. Several observers have recognised the potential of the world's religious traditions to offer the necessary inspiration, spiritual vision, ecological wisdom, ethical discernment, moral power, and hope to sustain an ecological transformation of the global economy and the widespread culture of consumerism. Religious traditions can offer the mystic motivation and enthusiasm that no secular or government initiatives can muster on such a wide scale. Indeed, if the cultural and economic habits of the world's 6.7 billion people are to be so radically transformed within a few decades, the role of faith communities will be crucial.

Given the historical impact of Christianity on those Western countries that have contributed most to environmental degradation, it should be evident that nothing less than an ecological reformation of Christianity itself is required. Christian ecotheology may be understood as a response to this challenge. Almost every aspect of Christian theology has come under the spotlight in this ecological reformation: Biblical Studies, Biblical hermeneutics, the history of Christianity, Christian doctrine, Christian virtues and values, preaching, ministry, pastoral care, ecclesial structures, Christian education, Christian ministries and mission, and theology of religions.

Norman Habel has done more than anyone else to employ an ecological hermeneutics in biblical interpretation—through the *Earth Bible* series, through the seminar on ecological hermeneutics under the umbrella of the Society for Biblical Literature, in a recent volume *Exploring Ecological Hermeneutics* and now, in *An Inconvenient Text*. Moreover, through his work on the Season of Creation he has also contributed to liturgical renewal and institutional transformation. Those of us working in academic and ecclesial contexts elsewhere in the world owe considerable gratitude to Norm Habel for his pioneering work in this regard, and for the relentless energy that he brings to this task.

It is probably fair to say that the ecological hermeneutics developed through the *Earth Bible* series and refined in this volume is one of the most radical forms of biblical hermeneutics imaginable. It deeply challenges readers to be suspicious about received anthropocentric views regarding the Bible, the Christian faith, ecclesial practices, and their own lifestyles. On this basis one may also explore the impact of other ecological 'sins' (such as alienation from the Earth community, and domination in the name of differences of gender, race, class, education and species) on the production and interpretation of biblical texts.

In this volume Habel tackles the problem of what he calls 'grey texts' in a typically uncompromising way. What should be done about those biblical texts that reveal an anthropocentric bias and that can only serve to legitimise human exploitation of otherkind? What about portraits of God that seem to devalue nature? His most vehement critique is aimed at interpretations of Genesis 1:26–28 as a benign model of environmental stewardship. Habel insists that this text portrays humans as the culmination of creation—and thereby devalues Earth and commissions humans to subdue Earth. In a similar way Habel shows that 'grey' texts depicting the 'mighty acts of God' and the conquest of the promised land condone the destruction of other creatures.

In response, Habel offers a constructive proposal, based on the core ecological insight that Earth is a precious living habitat, a fragile web of ecosystems, and a community of kin. In chapter 5, building on the six ecojustice principles articulated in the *Earth Bible* project, he proposes a method for dealing with grey texts in three steps: suspicion, identification with Earth, and retrieval of the voice of Earth in the text. This method is helpful in its simplicity and will certainly offer a frame of reference for others adopting an ecological hermeneutics in reading biblical texts to follow or to critique. Habel himself demonstrates how this method may be used creatively in order to read 'grey' texts against their grain. He does this on the basis of a Christological 'canon within the canon' (based on the Lutheran motto of *Was Christum treibet*) in which 'green' trajectories within New Testament texts are employed to critique 'grey' texts and to offer a new vision of service and solidarity in suffering.

In this book we are confronted not only with an inconvenient text that is both 'green' and 'grey', but also with an uncomfortable choice— to listen to the voice of Earth—and an unenviable task: 'to liberate ourselves from the power of those grey texts that have controlled our thinking, and through green texts to listen with empathy to cries of a suffering creation, and to discern God's presence there'. Habel calls a spade a spade; he refuses to accept easy compromises; he doesn't make the reader's task any easier. But, like a true prophet, he shows us the way towards a new ecological vision.

Ernst Conradie
University of the Western Cape, South Africa
November 2008

Contents

Introduction

An Inconvenient Truth confronted us with the cold reality of global warming and its consequences. Al Gore's bold production made it abundantly clear that the planet is in crisis. The Arctic and Antarctic regions of Earth are slowly melting and the oceans are rising. Toxic fumes are still choking our atmosphere. Old-growth forests continue to be cleared. Within twenty-five years, the greenhouse gases we emit are likely to double. The environmental crisis is escalating and to date relatively little has been done to stem the forces of global warming. There has been considerable talk about sustaining the life of the planet, but relatively little action.

In November 2007, we elected a new government in Australia. Within hours of being sworn into office, the Rudd Labor government endorsed the Kyoto protocol and said they would take the environmental crisis seriously. Various leaders of government, society and the church have declared their intention to face the cold reality exposed by *An Inconvenient Truth*. But the reality persists. Why?

Economically, companies view it as virtual suicide to declare a boycott on current fossil fuels or greenhouse emissions. Commitment to an ever-increasing production of goods and expenditure of wealth still controls our global economies. Australians, for example, bought more cars in 2007 than ever before. The story is similar is many other countries.

Socially, most groups are more concerned about sustaining their current lifestyles than about sustaining the ecosystems of the planet. 'Sustainability' has been appropriated by the propaganda machines of our society: it has come to mean 'sustaining our affluent lifestyles' rather than working to counter the ecological upheavals of our planet and sustaining a balanced ecology. We are not yet serious about adjusting our ways of living for the sake of the planet—or even for future generations living on the planet.

Geographically, we can point to a range of countries that have been invaded by colonial powers who believed that it was God's will that they conquer pagan lands, harness the forces of nature, introduce agriculture as a divine mandate, and establish a set of Judeo-Christian values that view parts of creation as domains to be colonised. The founding belief of many nations of the world—both old and new—is that they have a divine right to dominate nature.

And, it seems to me, we have yet to internalise psychologically either the emerging worldview informed by ecology or the seriousness of the ecological crisis. We watch Al Gore's scenario and walk away—as is the case with any other movie—moved but moving on! There is an increased awareness of environmental issues but observable changes in our environments—whether sea levels or consumption levels—are minimal. As a species, we are rarely shocked into action!

Historically, there are many factors that have contributed to our current worldview: our orientation to this planet and life on the planet. Our values have been formulated over generations by a range of social, political and religious forces. One of these factors, I would argue, is the value system which we have inherited from Christianity—or more particularly, from the Bible. We have been conditioned, in part, by *an inconvenient text*: the Bible.

More than forty years ago, Lynn White Jr. wrote his famous article entitled 'The historical roots of our ecological crisis'[1] Santmire suggests that this article might well be compared to Luther's '95 Theses'[2]. Some theologians have forcefully protested against White's claim that the biblical text—especially the reference to 'dominion' over nature—has contributed significantly to the senseless exploitation of nature for the sole benefit of humans.

> **After exploring ecology and the Bible for more than twenty years, I have come to the conclusion that White was probably on the right track. The Bible, as a major force in the Western Christian tradition, is not obviously green and has certainly not been read by Christians—whether scholars or laity—as a work that immediately connects us personally with nature. In the past, the Bible has generally not made Christians green in their attitude to creation—just the opposite!**

There are indeed exciting sections of the Scriptures from which we can retrieve voices that connect us with creation in a positive way; *The Earth*

---

1. Lynn White Jr, 'The historical roots of our ecological crisis', in *Science*, 155 (1967): 1203–7.
2. H Paul Santmire, *Nature Reborn: The Ecological and Cosmic Promise of Christian Theology* (Minneapolis: AugsburgFortress, 2000), 11.

Bible project that I initiated demonstrates that fact. There are texts that record nature mourning and rejoicing; there are texts that celebrate the presence of God in Earth rather than in heaven. Much of the Bible, however, has been used to justify our domination, devaluation and destruction of the planet.

The Bible is *an inconvenient text.*

In this study, I first intend to explore a selection of the key passages from the Bible that have provided justification for the way we have wounded and abused our planet. My hope is that biblical scholars, church leaders, and interested students of our modern world will face this negative force in our history and recognise the need to change our orientation—both to the way we read the Bible and towards the biblical values that shape our lives.

While there are numerous texts from the Bible that could be examined in this context, I will focus on three crucial areas that have influenced our values. The first texts are those that indicate directives given by God as to how human beings are to control nature; the second group highlights those mighty acts of God that include the destruction of parts of nature; and the third set refers to traditions associated with the divine gift of a promised land.

As a way of distinguishing these texts from others in my analysis, I refer to these problematic passages as 'grey' texts. These are texts in which nature is devalued either at the hands of humans or God. As I analyse these texts initially, I will pursue a reading which demonstrates their grey character: I will clarify the way they devalue nature, focus on human interests, and suppress the character or voice of Earth in the text.

It is not sufficient, of course, to uncover the demons in our past. We also need to have a vision of how things might change. Basic to creating such a vision is a radical re-orientation towards our planet. Or, if you prefer, we need to accept ecology as a key dimension of an emerging view of the natural world, rather than just another discipline like botany or chemistry or theology. From within that emerging ecological worldview, we are challenged to read the Bible, do theology, reform worship, and then to confront the political forces of our times.

One of the movements seeking to achieve this end is *The Green Seminary Initiative* based in Chicago (see www.webofcreation.org). The goal of this initiative is to promote the care of creation as an integral part of the seminary curriculum and parish education. A second movement is *The Season of Creation* which seeks to green our worship (see www.seasonofcreation.com). I would also extend the challenge further and pursue what some Catholic documents have called 'an ecological conversion' as an integral part of our Christian faith.

Accordingly, the second stage of this book is designed to re-position our faith within an emerging worldview informed by ecology, to challenge our use of the Bible as a vehicle to support the status quo, and to consider a radical re-reading of the text.

> **The question we face: is a green reading of the Bible is possible; or do 'grey' texts and 'grey' attitudes still control our orientation to creation and nature in the Bible?**

To be green, I would argue, is to have empathy with Earth. And that empathy is grounded in the reality that I and every other human being are children of Earth. For millions of years, all forms of life—including humans—have been nurtured by the elements and impulses of Earth. I am an integral part of the living web called creation. I taste the same salt water as the dolphin. I depend on the trees for oxygen. I celebrate life with the blue wren in my garden. And I suffer with the soil when it is polluted by nuclear waste.

The task before me is to translate that empathy into a fresh way of reading of the text. I adopt this approach—not simply because of the growing environmental crisis—but because I have become conscious that I am one with Earth in a way that was not fully apparent in the past.

To be grey, on the other hand, is to be anthropocentric and to view nature primarily as a resource for humans to exploit. Being grey means that as a human I am superior to nature and have the right to colonise creation, to appropriate this gift as a means of furthering economic progress. The rights of humans always come first. The interests of humans always come first. And the future of humans always comes first.

Being green is not, as some have suggested, a backhanded way of protecting the interests of humans. Earth and all life on Earth have intrinsic value. My concern is not simply the future of my grandchildren; my concern is also for this planet called Earth.

To be green **is to have empathy with Earth because I know myself as a child of Earth.** To be grey **is to view nature as a resource for humans to exploit because I assume humans are superior to the rest of nature.**

Before articulating an alternative way of reading a text—however grey that text may be—I need to reflect briefly on the emerging view of the natural world that an ecological perspective is beginning to create in our society. I will locate this emerging worldview over against worldviews of the past that have become obsolete and anachronistic; worldviews that were often justified on the basis of the Bible. This emerging worldview will take into account the reality of Earth as a living planet, a fragile web of interconnected forces and a community of kin. I will also summarise the challenge that this worldview presents when we dare to consider the key texts under discussion from this perspective.

Of course, numerous biblical scholars have tackled recently the grey texts under analysis. At appropriate points in the text I will cite a number of these studies. For many of us, their approaches may seem to offer an adequate response to the challenge posed by these grey texts. For some of us, however, the way we read the Bible remains a problem as we seek to adopt Earth-friendly, green responses to the current environmental crisis. Interpreters, it seems, are only too ready to compromise the text in the interests of accepted theology, church politics, or even popular opinion about the importance of sustaining our lifestyle. We need to ask whether—and how—we can legitimately green our study of the Scriptures.

The green approach being espoused in this volume and elsewhere takes into account the bias of past approaches which persist in reading the text predominantly from the perspective of human beings—that is, they are anthropocentric readings. Green readers are now asking how we might read the text from the perspective of Earth and the Earth community. We are exploring ways of readings demonstrating empathy for Earth.

A significant prototype in this endeavour is that of feminist interpreters who read from their experience and perspective as women. Another model is that of scholars who pursue a postcolonial approach, recognising that in the past we have read the Bible from the perspective of the invaders and the powerful rather than from that of the indigenous peoples or the poor. In a sense, creation has become a domain to be conquered. How do we read from the perspective of a conquered domain of creation?

Some scholars, such as Sallie McFague, argue that the current environmental crisis is also a theological crisis. Her book, *A New Climate for Theology*[3], challenges us to read the Bible and our Christian heritage from the context of a planet facing the disaster of global warming and to articulate a new theology with a genuine empathy for Earth.

Three of the key questions I pose in this volume are these:

- Are there texts in the Bible where the voices of Earth and Earth community are present, but have been ignored because of the mindset of past interpreters?
- How might we retrieve the voices of Earth and Earth community that have been suffocated by human authors and readers who focus first and foremost on human interests?
- What happens when we also read with empathy for Earth rather than from the perspective of the welfare of humans?

I will articulate a radical new way of reading involving three steps: suspicion, identification, retrieval. To demonstrate how this approach differs from preceding approaches, I will apply this way of reading the text to a selection of grey texts discussed in the first three chapters, texts relating to the mandate to dominate, the mighty acts of God and the promised land. This application, while brief, illustrates what it means to identify with Earth as a character and voice in the text, even if that voice has been suppressed.

In the final three chapters, as I explore the application of green principles to texts I will also seek to retrieve green voices located in parallel texts. At the end of each chapter, I will also explore whether there are key texts in the New Testament that are unequivocally green and could provide a basis for choosing the green texts over the grey texts. In the conclusion, I focus on this choice—an uncomfortable choice between passages in an inconvenient text, the Christian Bible.

The plan of this volume then is:

- analysis of **three sets of grey texts**, focusing on the mandate to dominate, the mighty acts of God and the promised land (chapters 1–3);
- discussion of **the emerging world view** about our planet that now

---

3. Sallie McFague, *A New Climate for Theology. God, the World and Global Warming* (Minneapolis: Fortress, 2008).

informs the way we view reality—as we read the text (chapter 4);
*   introduction to a new **green approach to reading** the text (chapter 5);
*   **re-reading** of the three sets of texts analysed in chapters 1–3, using this approach and taking into account **supplementary texts** as well as New Testament contexts (chapters 6–8);
*   **conclusion—an uncomfortable choice** between grey and green texts and consideration of **an unenviable task**.

I recognise that more academic versions of some of what I have written here have appeared in various scholarly journals, as the bibliography demonstrates. These articles, however, are often inaccessible to general readers. I hope that what I have re-formulated here illustrates the significance of this approach as we face the current environmental crisis and the need to green biblical studies in our seminaries and churches. The Bible will probably remain an inconvenient text in the current global climate. The question before us, however, is how we face that reality as we pursue green initiatives in our worship, our lives and our study of the Bible. For responsible Christians, this challenging question cannot be avoided: Is a green reading of the Bible possible?

In recent writings numerous scholars have sought to demonstrate the green credentials of God as Creator. Few, however, have sought to face the fact that the portraits of God, especially in the Old Testament, are often grey rather than green.

1

The Mandate to Dominate

'God intended the land for sheep, not for trees'
Hamilton Spectator, **1879**

Refusing to be conscripted into the Prussian army, my great grandfather Wilhelm Habel immigrated to Australia from Germany in the 1840s and established a farm between two lakes, one saltwater and the other freshwater. His farm was on the saltwater lake. The freshwater lake, which was less than half a mile away, had been cleared of all trees up to the water's edge. Wilhelm, who had a genuine bond with nature, decided to plant native Australian trees around the second lake and restore the lake to life. Within a week, the local farmers had pulled up every tree. The local newspaper reported that 'God intended the land for sheep not for trees'. Not to be denied, Wilhelm was eventually elected to the local council and had the land around the lake preserved as a natural park. One letter to the editor declared this action to be 'an extravagant appropriation of crown lands'.

The attitude of these Australian farmers is typical of the way settlers throughout the Western world viewed their relationship with the land. It was God's will that they should clear the land and make it productive. It was God's will that the trees of the forests should be felled and make way for human progress. It was God's will that human beings transform the landscape into farms, mines and roads. After all, the wild west had to be tamed, the outback had to be conquered and nature had to be harnessed!

What were the sources of this belief that nature be harnessed in this way? Sheep are important, but why, in our Christian heritage, does the human drive to transform the landscape for human ends take precedence over even the God-given order of creation?

One source, I suggest, was an inconvenient text called the Bible!

An underlying source of this popular belief seems to be the mandate to dominate in Gen 1:26–28. I recognise that there may have been many other factors involved in the development of our Western drive to exploit nature, and I appreciate that the Bible has been used in many ways to

1

support many different causes and attitudes. However, we also need to acknowledge that there has been a long line of interpreters who have found that the Genesis 1 mandate to dominate, and similar biblical texts, are grounds for humans harnessing and exploiting nature.

I also recognise also that many scholars in recent years have sought to soften the mandate to dominate in Genesis by interpreting it as a compassionate commission to sustain the planet. The text itself and its interpretation over the centuries, however, leave little doubt in my mind that the Genesis text is indeed a mandate to dominate. The vast majority of interpretations over the centuries are anthropocentric: they are human centred, viewing humans as the culmination of creation and thereby devaluing any other subjects in the text.

Gen 1:26–28, I would argue, is a grey text—a text that is ecologically destructive, devaluing Earth and offering humans a God-given right to harness nature.

The text reads:

> Then God said, 'Let us make humankind in our image, according to our likeness; and let them have dominion over the fish of the sea and over the birds of the air, and over the cattle, and over all the wild animals of the Earth and over every creeping things that creeps upon the Earth.' So God created humankind in his image, in the image of God he created them, male and female he created them. God blessed them, and said to them, 'be fruitful and multiply, and fill the Earth and subdue it; and have dominion over the fish of the sea and over the birds of the air and over every living thing that moves upon the Earth'.
> (Gen 1:26–28)

There are three dimensions of this passage that make it grey: the image of God; the mandate to dominate living creatures; and the commission to subdue Earth. I will discuss these three dimensions in detail below.

The Genesis context

On each of the preceding days of creation in Genesis 1, the narrator simply announces the creative impulse as a self-reflection of God. God says, 'Let there be light' and there is light. God says, 'Let Earth bring forth' and Earth brings forth. The context of Genesis 1 is a primal narrative in which Earth is a major character who emerges from out of the deep on the third day[1].

With the creation of humans, however, a new element is introduced which signals a creation of a different order. God, in concert with unidentified others, says 'Let **us** make…'. The decision to create humans is a shared decision presumably with a heavenly council. This radical change in God's way of operating highlights the significance of this act as climactic when viewed from an anthropocentric perspective where the interests of humans are primary.

The processes employed by God in the creation of the domains of nature normally involved the separation of existing parts of the primal world consisting of darkness and water, or the generation of a new domain from an existing domain. Thus light is separated from darkness, waters are separated from waters, and day is separated from night on days one, two, three and four. On days three, five and six, fauna and flora are generated from the land, the waters and the atmosphere. Earth is a partner with God in producing these creatures. They are Earth-born![2]

The image of God

With the creation of humankind, however, no connection is made with any existing domain of the primal or created order. Humans do not emerge from an existing domain of nature as do other living creatures. Instead, humans are made by God using a totally different process. They are made using an image (Hebrew *tselem*). Other living creatures are Earth-born, while humans are image-modelled. In this grey text, humans are **not** portrayed as part of Earth or originating from Earth in any way

Interpretations of the image of God (*imago dei*) in this text are legion and cannot be explored in detail here. A long tradition that goes back to figures like Philo, who was influenced by dualistic Platonic thought, promotes the idea that the image refers to a non-physical dimension of humans: mind, reason, consciousness or a spiritual core[3]. The usual meaning of the Hebrew word for image (*tselem*), however, is something

---

1. Norman Habel, 'Geophany: the Earth Story in Genesis One', in Norman Habel & Shirley Wurst, eds, *The Earth Story in Genesis* (The Earth Bible 2; Sheffield: Sheffield Academic Press, 2000), 34–48.
2. Habel, 'Geophany', 34–48.
3. David Fergusson, *The Cosmos and the Creator. An Introduction to the Theology of Creation* (London: SPCK, 1998), 13.

concrete and visible, for example, a statue of a deity (2Kgs 11:18; Dan 3:1) or a picture on a wall (Ezek 23:14).

A careful reading of the text reveals that the usual Hebrew verb for 'create' (*bara'*) is not used for the creation of humans. Instead, like an artisan, God 'makes' (`*asah*) a God-image as one would make a model. The same verb is used for 'making images' in several other texts. The Philistine priests, for example, give the order to 'make images of the mice' that were ravaging the land (1Sam 6:5; cf Ezek 7:20).

Probably, for readers in the ancient world, the use of the same verb for humans being made in the image of God and the making of physical images would have suggested that human beings were believed to represent God—that is, to 'image God'. The image of the king was frequently erected to announce to the world that this territory was under the rule of that king; the image represented the king. In the same way, humans created in the image of the deity-as-king would be viewed as royal representatives of the ruling deity[4]. As representatives of the divine ruler, the humans could exercise power over nature and conquer it as any king of the ancient world might do.

In numerous readings of this text, however, biblical scholars and theologians have tended to avoid recognising the very physical dimension of the divine action; rather, they discern a higher dimension for humans that somehow makes human beings belong to an even higher order. As a consequence, traditional readings of the text have fostered a strong anthropocentric approach. That is, these readings have fostered a tendency for humans to play God by identifying with a dimension of God that they believe they can emulate or express. Sibley Towner goes so far as to claim this text makes humans 'clones of God' and 'prime ministers of the King of the universe'—but without the right to 'play God'[5]. His reading is boldly anthropocentric. Dean McBride even speaks of humans as the presence of God in the cosmos. He writes[6]:

> The particular purpose of their creation is 'theophanic': to represent or mediate the sovereign presence of the deities

---

4. Gerhard von Rad, *Genesis. A Commentary* (Philadelphia: Westminster, 1961), 58.
5. Sibley Towner, 'The Future of Nature', in *Interpretation* 50 (1996), 35.
6. Dean S. McBride, 'Divine Protocol: Genesis 1.1–2.3 as Prologue to the Pentateuch', in William Brown & S Dean McBride, eds, *God Who Creates* (Grand Rapids: Eerdmanns, 2000), 16.

within the central nave of the cosmic temple just as cult images were supposed to do in conventional sanctuaries.

> **Whatever the precise interpretation of the image of God that church leaders or scholars may have endorsed in the past, it has almost always provided a justification for proclaiming the superiority of human beings over all other animate or inanimate domains of Earth. The image of God clearly separates humans from the rest of nature, gives them a status that justifies their claim to be superior beings and, in so doing, devalues the rest of creation.**

The mandate to dominate

Precisely because human beings are made in the image of God, they are given the mandate to dominate all living creatures. Lest there be any question about what creatures are involved, the text delineates a wide range of representative living things: fish, birds, domestic animals, wild animals and creeping things. Humans are given the authority to rule as God's representative over all living things in nature.

As Towner[7] points out, the logic of the text is clear: 'Let us make humankind (*adam*) in our image, according to our likeness, *so that* they may have dominion'. Being made in God's image is not associated with the capacity of humans to communicate with God in some way, but with the role of exercising dominion over creatures and subduing Earth.

> **The stance of this grey text is quite explicit: humans are created in God's image *so that* they may have dominion!**

In recent discussions about this text, there has been considerable debate about the Hebrew term *rada* which has been rendered 'rule' or 'have dominion'. Normally *rada* is what kings and taskmasters do (1Kgs 4:24; 5:16): dominate their subjects and their enemies. As it stands, the text is decidedly grey; it declares that humans are given a mandate to dominate all other living creatures. That function, it would seem, devalues these creatures and justifies forceful human acts of subjugation.

In this text, there is no indication of kinship between human beings and any other living beings, nor any connection between humans and

---

7. Towner, 'Nature', 348.

Earth as the domain from which they are made or emerge. Humans and Earth are represented as separate, belonging to two discrete domains!

The god-images known as humans are blessed like other creatures with the power of reproduction. For humans, however, this blessing also means a capacity to 'fill' Earth and so 'subdue' it. The act of filling Earth suggests that Earth is the domain where humans are to rule. Fish may fill the seas (Gen 1:22) but humans fill Earth, the domain where the Earth-born creatures already live. 'Filling' Earth sounds like a takeover. This is confirmed with the final mandate: 'subdue' Earth!

The Hebrew verb *kabash* ('subdue') has all the connotations of heavy-handed control. 'Crushing under foot' (Mic 7:19) and 'subjugating' the land of Canaan (Josh 18:1) are typical images that reflect the oppressive dimension of the verb and its consistency with the verb *rada*, to rule. In addition, this verb is associated with subduing a woman to rape her (Esth 7:9; Neh 5:5), an association that clearly reflects a connotation of forced domination of Earth. Of course, the belief that humans have 'raped Earth' has been acknowledged by many well into the twentieth century.

In a detailed critical scholarly analysis of the image of God in Gen 1:26–8, Garr[8] maintains

> *kabash* (subdue) is a harsh term that empowers, in this case, human beings to control, occupy, and subjugate a vast area by an exercise of mighty force. The 'image' entitles humankind to achieve decisive victory over the entire natural world. Stated differently, humankind will act like a victorious king over a conquered land.

Daniel Hillel is a *bone fide* ecologist. In an appendix to his recent work *The Natural History of the Bible,* Hillel recognises that this text can be construed as 'a divine ordination of humans to dominate Earth and to use every nonliving and living thing on it for their own purposes, without restraint or reservation'[9].

---

8. Randall W Garr, *In His Own Image and Likeness. Humanity, Divinity, and Monotheism* (Leiden: Brill, 2003), 171.
9. Daniel Hillel, *The Natural History of the Bible. An Environmental Exploration of the Hebrew Scriptures* (New York: Columbia University Press, 2006), 242.

> Earth in this grey text is a domain to be overpowered by those creatures who bear God's image. The mandate to 'subdue' provides a justification for de-powering and devaluing not only Earth creatures but also Earth itself.

Reinforcing the mandate

We might well expect, after the debacle of the flood and the declaration that humans are corrupt and sinful, that their status as creatures bearing God's image would be downgraded. On the contrary, after the flood subsides and before God makes a promise to humans, animals and Earth never again to destroy Earth with a flood, God reinforces the mandate for humans to dominate the animal world, albeit with certain modifications.

Humans are to continue multiplying and filling Earth in order to control it. Their relationship with living creatures, however, changes somewhat: now it is made explicit that all living creatures will be terrified of their human overlords. God's edict:

> The fear and dread of you shall rest on every animal of the earth, and on every bird of the air, and on everything that creeps on the ground and on all the fish of the sea; into your hand they are delivered.
> (Gen 9:2)

This edict is grey indeed. The reinforcement of the mandate is clear: 'Into your hand I have delivered them!'. To be 'in the hand' of someone is to be under his or her control. Humans are given unequivocal dominion of the animal world—a dominion that also reflects an increased alienation between humans and other living creatures.

This increased alienation seems decidedly unfair. Why should these creatures suffer additional anxiety in their relationships with humans? Humans were the primary source of the corruption of life that led to the flood in the first place. Yet, in the wake of the flood, the relative worth and standing of nonhuman creatures has dropped even further.

From the perspective of the wider Earth community this mandate seems, once more, to be an unjust decree from God. The hierarchy of relationships established in Gen 1:26–28 now becomes entrenched. God is apparently concerned first of all with the role of humans rather than justice for nonhuman creatures. The mandate to dominate from Genesis 1 is here given God's seal of approval.

In addition, this mandate is now the basis for killing animals for food; previously, it seems, both animals and humans ate vegetation (Gen 1:29–20). The blood, however, is not to be eaten: it is to be acknowledged as belonging to God. The sharp differentiation between humans and other living creatures is further endorsed by the fact the humans are not to be killed like animals. Why? Precisely because humans are made in the image of God! To kill a human is to destroy an image of God!

> **The image of God which justifies the mandate to dominate in Genesis 1 persists in the post-Flood world of new beginnings and reinforces the superiority of humans over all animal life.**

Celebrating the mandate

The full force of the mandate to dominate is felt in a widely celebrated poem, namely, Psalm 8. This psalm is popular in Christian worship and the inspiration for quite a number of chants and hymns. Through such repetition, the mandate to dominate continues to be celebrated in the worship—and faith—of many Christian communities.

The relevant section of the Psalm 8 reads:

> You have made them (humans) a little lower than God,
>   and crowned them with glory and honour.
> You have given them **dominion** over the work of your hands;
>   you have put all things under their feet,
>   all sheep and oxen and also the beasts of the field,
>   the birds of the air and the fish of the sea,
>   whatever passes along the paths of the seas.
>   (Ps 8:5–8)

As with the mandate to dominate in Gen 1:26–28, in Psalm 8 humans are depicted as connected with God in a special way—and disconnected from the rest of creation. The royal language elevates humans to the status of lordship over the natural world. Their dominion extends not only to all kinds of living things on the land, in the sea and in the air, but also to all the work of God's hands. Nothing is excluded: humans reign supreme over all of creation in Psalm 8!

This celebration of the mandate to dominate is a grey text indeed.

The case for human lordship is not argued, but is taken for granted and made the subject of joyful celebration. In so doing, I would argue, the natural world is again devalued: nature is placed 'under the feet' of humans, and thereby assumes the position of a slave or a defeated foe. What could be more degrading!

Some scholars have sought to soften the harsh role of humans announced in this text. Limburg[10], for example, attempts an ecological reading that focuses on the royal responsibilities of humankind who are to reign like shepherds. But as Carley[11] and others have shown, the role of kings—who were often called shepherds in the ancient world—was brutal and far from caring. To be under the feet of kings and to lick their feet (Ps 72:8) is hardly an expression of Earth-care.

Admittedly, the author of the book of Job dares to undermine the text of Psalm 8 somewhat by declaring that humans, with their sad and empty lives, are the real slaves on Earth (Job 7:1–2). God, he insists, sets God's mind on humans every morning to harass and hound them (Job 7:17–19). Job's experience of reality is precisely the opposite of the relationship with God depicted in Psalm 8. Job also accuses God of using his wisdom to 'overthrow Earth' (Job 12:13–15). Job's 'alternative orientation', however, was generally ignored in Christian worship. Celebrating the mandate to dominate in work and worship was the prevailing mindset.

The challenge

Whether we like it or not, and whether or not we wish to modify the reading of these texts in some way, the mandate to dominate remains a serious grey text in the Bible. My reading, I would contend, is an honest analysis of the text reflecting the anthropocentric way most interpreters over the centuries have viewed its message and meaning. I believe we need to face the force of this passage and ask ourselves how we plan to deal with the challenge it poses in the current environmental crisis. I believe we need to avoid the temptation of more recent interpreters to re-read these texts as if the mandate to dominate was really a way

---

10. James Limburg, 'Who Cares for the Earth? Psalm Eight and the Environment', in AJ Hultgren et al, eds, *All Things New* (WWS Series 1; St Paul: Lutheran Theological Seminary, 1991), 50.
11. Keith Carley, 'An Apology for Domination', in Norman Habel & Shirley Wurst, eds, *Readings from the Perspective of Earth* (The Earth Bible 1; Sheffield: Sheffield Academic Press, 2000), 119.

of saying humans need to sustain the planet or be compassionate with creation. In chapter 6 I explore what fresh insights a green reading of this text in context might reveal.

Meanwhile, the mandate to dominate remains a crucial grey passage in an inconvenient text called the Bible.

The mandate to dominate and subdue Earth was a living force among early settlers. A nineteenth century poem by Frank Masters (an elder in a Christian congregation in Driver River, South Australia) 'The Pioneers'[12] clearly illustrates the mandate to dominate:

> **It was the over-flow Westward of the mainland expansion**
> **That surged first to the plains of this goodly land,**
> **Then tackled scrub (clearing) with roller and axe,**
> **An exodus obedient to great Biblical command:**
> **'Be fruitful and multiply and replenish the earth**
> **And subdue it!' with its accompanied blessing.**

---

12. Janice Clements, *Arno Bay and District 1883–1983* (Arno Bay Centenary Committee, 1982), 195.

2

The Mighty Acts of God

'When the rainbow is in the clouds I will see it and remember.'
Genesis 9:16

The elusive nature of the rainbow has long fascinated me. In the early 1980s I would drive to the university and park my car facing into the West. Often in winter there would be a rainbow or two suspended in the clouds to the West—a sign, I supposed, to jog God's memory.

On one occasion, as I drove to my usual parking spot, I was astounded to see a white rainbow—or to be more precise, there was a bright white arch across the clouds precisely where the rainbow normally hung. What was happening? The science lecturers at the university said I was 'seeing things' and would not believe me. What would God be thinking if the 'remind me' rainbow suddenly turned white? What kind of twist in the ecosystem produces a white rainbow?

According to Genesis 9, the rainbow was created to remind God that God has a covenant with all creatures on Earth and with Earth itself. A basic promise within that covenant is that God will never again destroy Earth with a flood—a promise that apparently represents a reversal of God's previous way of operating.

Hans Walter Wolff, a mentor of mine, used to say that the rainbow was originally understood as God's bow: a weapon God had hung up in the sky to signify peace with Earth.

Students of the Bible have, in the context of the environmental crisis, cited this covenant as a clear indication of God's continued concern for creation and God's compassion for Earth. The inference is that God has a covenant bond with Earth and consequently that God places a high value on Earth and the domains of nature. A further inference is that humans should follow in God's wake and reflect a similar covenantal attitude of care for creation—whatever the colour of the rainbow in the sky!

Does the story of God's relationship with the domains of Earth in subsequent texts of the Old Testament support this reading? Does God's covenant with creation restrain God from inflicting further destructive

11

acts on Earth? Or does Earth hear God's promise like that of a well-meaning spouse: 'I will never abuse you again, my darling, I promise'? Does God's treatment of Earth provide a model of care for creation that humans are encouraged to follow? Or does this inconvenient text called the Bible offer further divine precedents that might well justify corresponding human deeds of destruction?

Before exploring God's typical interventions in history that impinge on the domains of Earth, it is informative to examine the flood narrative itself and explore precisely how God relates to Earth and the creatures of Earth in this text[1].

Mighty acts of God in the flood

Sinful humans—death to all animals!
Two discrete introductions to the flood narrative offer two quite different rationales for the flood. The first, in Gen 6:5–8, depicts God surveying the behaviour of human beings on Earth. Their minds, it seems, have become obsessed with wickedness—or as the narrator says: 'every inclination of the thoughts of their hearts was only evil continually' (Gen 6:5). Understandably, this scenario causes God grief and anguish. 'The Lord', continues the narrator, 'changes his mind that he made humankind on the Earth'. The human experiment has failed!

The narrative has followed a logical and balanced progression to this point. The expected outcome of God's distress is that God would punish humankind—in this case by using a flood. There is, however, an unexpected development, a subversive dimension to the story that may alert the reader to consider another agenda. God decides not only to obliterate all people on Earth because of their evil ways, but also the animals, birds and reptiles created with humankind. In this plan, human beings are obsessed with sin and must be removed from their earthly home; but the rest of the Earth community is likewise condemned to oblivion:

---

1. See Norman Habel, 'What Kind of God would Destroy Earth Anyway? An Ecojustice Reading of the Flood Narrative', in Wesley Bergen & Emin Siedlecki, eds, *Voyages in Unchartered Waters. Essays in the Theory and Practice* of *Biblical Interpretation* (Sheffield: Sheffield Phoenix Press, 2006a), 203–11.

> And the Lord was sorry that he had made humankind on the earth, and it grieved him to his heart. So the Lord said, 'I will blot out from the earth the human beings I have created—people **together with** animals and creeping things and birds of the air, for I am sorry that I made them'.
> (Gen 6:6–7)

Why blot out all living creatures? The animals and birds have done nothing wrong. The various living species of the wild are totally innocent. Yet, they too will die. Nonhuman life seems to have no intrinsic worth in God's eyes. God seems to be obsessed with human beings and their ways. All living things are apparently disposable, just a part of the human experiment.

Corrupt ways—corrupt Earth!
In the second introduction (Gen 6:11–13), the portrayal of conditions is very different. In this scenario Earth is seen as 'corrupted' or 'spoiled' and filled with 'violence'. According to this version, all flesh has become corrupted—not just human flesh. The corruption, however, is not caused by Earth itself, but by all flesh corrupting its way[2] of being on Earth. In this version, other life than human life has also become corrupt or spoilt in some way.

The logical divine verdict, in the light of this chaotic situation, may be to start again by giving each creature a new nature that is not so easily corrupted. But once again, the forces of divine destruction reach beyond the culprits and include the innocent: God explicitly plans to destroy all these corrupted creatures 'along with Earth'. Earth—the home and source of all flesh—and all its inhabitants will be destroyed. Earth is destined for destruction even though Earth has not been the cause of the disorder. Earth seems to have no intrinsic value; it can be annihilated willy-nilly along with the rest of life, as this grey text confirms:

---

2. The 'way' (*derek*) is a technical term in Hebrew Wisdom literature referring to the 'essential character' of a creature or domain of creation eg 'the way of the ant' (Prov 6:6); 'the way of an eagle' (Prov 30:19). When the creature's 'way' is corrupted, the creature is not behaving as created. See Norman Habel, 'The Implications of God Discovering Wisdom in Earth', in Ellen van Wolde, ed, *Job 28: Cognition and Context* (Leiden: Brill, 2003), 281–98.

> And God said to Noah, 'I have determined to make an end of all flesh, for the Earth is filled with violence because of them; now I am going to destroy them **along with** Earth'. (Gen 6:13)

While the pre-flood worlds portrayed in each of these rationales is very different, they have one significant feature in common: the divine hand of destruction reaches beyond the guilty to embrace an innocent party. In the first scenario the innocent are the living creatures of Earth; in the second Earth suffers unjustly. We may well ask: is there anything green about the actions of this God? And are the ways of this God the ways humans have, quite understandably, followed in history?

The mighty acts of God in the flood narrative are decidedly grey rather than green: innocent animals and an innocent Earth experience destruction at God's hand.

Two compensations after the flood

No more cursing of the ground

The gory and glorious details of the flood event itself will not be analysed in detail here. Our concern is to ascertain how God, after the flood, deals with the acts of destruction that God has inflicted on all life on Earth and on Earth itself.

The flood is portrayed as a return to the pre-creation scene where Earth is submerged beneath primal waters. Now the cosmic waters above the sky descend and the subterranean waters of the deep return to submerge everything. Earth, as we know it, is destroyed and returned to its primal state—with the exception that in place of a hovering spirit on the face of the deep there is a bobbing boat.

The closure of the flood narrative in Gen 8:20–22 corresponds to the first of the two introductory rationales. Noah responds to his release from the ark with a grand and glorious sacrifice: he kills one of each clean animal and bird. All clean species, it seems, are represented on this bloody altar of thanksgiving. God, in turn, responds to the overwhelming aroma of this event and starts talking to the divine self.

According to the biblical narrator, the delighted Lord says to the divine self: 'I will never again curse the ground because of humankind!'. Why? 'Because the inclination of the human heart is evil from youth!' And the divine soliloquy continues: 'I will never again destroy every living creature as I have done' (Gen 8:21).

There are several significant confessions in this soliloquy. First and foremost, God confesses that God's cursing of the ground was, in fact, a response to human sin. The ground (*adamah*) is the innocent victim: the ground suffered at God's hands because of what humans did.

God cursed the ground! The curse was not confined to the human culprits. While the context suggests that the flood is the immediate curse in question, there seems to be an echo of Gen 3:17 where it is specifically the ground (*adamah*) rather than Earth that is cursed because of Adam's sin. In effect, God is confessing that Earth, and—in particular the ground—has suffered innocently at God's hands. Not only the living creatures of the ground, but also the ground—the very source of life—are cursed by God.

In this version of the flood narrative, the ground is not able to save the creatures she has spawned. All but a few drown in the flood. God has cursed the mother with the children.

Humans are obsessive creatures—they love to sin. If God were to perpetuate a curse policy, Earth would be repeatedly under threat because humans are always bent on evil. The ground, however, gets a reprieve—a kind of backhanded declaration of innocence!

The form of this reprieve is a promise that the seasons of the year will not be disrupted by curses like the flood. The cycles of life can continue with the cycle of the seasons. The animals also get a reprieve. God promises that they too will never again be the innocent victims of a curse at God's hands.

In the history of humankind that follows the flood, is this promise kept? Does the God portrayed here assiduously avoid cursing, killing or harming the animal world because of the sins of humans? Or does the policy of collateral damage as punishment for human sin continue in nature?

No more corrupting of Earth

The second conclusion to the Flood narrative has a decidedly different focus. The emphasis is not on a promise never to impose any future curses on nature, but rather on a covenant binding God to the natural world in a powerful way.

There is a significant progression in the apparently repetitive announcement of this covenant. First, God promises a covenant with Noah's family, his descendants and all living creatures. Second, God incorporates in this covenant a promise that God will never again destroy all life with a flood nor will there be a flood to destroy Earth. Third, a rainbow is introduced as a sign of this covenant that is now extended to be 'a covenant between me and Earth'. And finally, God promises to use the rainbow as a sign to remember this covenant never to send another flood to destroy all flesh. Or in the words of a penitent spouse: 'Look, my darling, now I have something to help me remember my promise not to abuse you again'.

A key term throughout this version of the flood narrative is the verb for 'corrupt' (*shachat*). This verb is the same verb that appears in the introduction to this version. The Earth was declared corrupt (*shachat*) because all flesh had corrupted (*shachat*) their ways on Earth. God then does the same thing that all flesh has done. All flesh has corrupted its ways on Earth, so God 'corrupts' all flesh and Earth. God completes the corruption process.

Is this a case of the punishment fitting the crime as Patrick Miller suggests. Miller quite rightly focuses on the thematic force of this verb (*shachat*) [3]. It seems beneath God, however, to punish humans and all of life with the very corruption that God condemns. God, it seems, stoops to a human level of corruption! What Miller omits to mention is the fact that God admits corrupting Earth itself, not only all flesh on Earth. Earth has been corrupted by human violence, not by its own actions. Why then should God go even further and corrupt Earth with the forces of a primordial flood? Why is Earth, the innocent party, treated so badly by God?

> **The only compensation for Earth is a promise that God will never again corrupt Earth, a promise that embraces a divine admission that God was the culprit. But does God keep this promise? Does the history of God's dealing with humanity in subsequent texts demonstrate that God protects Earth and the domains of Earth rather than imposing curses or acts of destruction? Are future mighty acts of God green?**

Mighty acts of God in the exodus from Egypt

The exodus of the Israelites from Egypt is a pivotal event in the Hebrew Scriptures. This event is recorded in both narrative and poetic form

---

3. Patrick Miller, *Genesis 1–11: Studies in Structure and Theme* (JSOT Testament Supplement Series 8; Sheffield: Sheffield Academic Press, 1978), 34.

(Exodus 14–15). The God of the exodus is proclaimed as a God who keeps promises, identifies with the underdog and offers the hope of liberation and freedom for all who are oppressed. The God of the exodus is at the heart of the so-called history of salvation tradition which identified the biblical God as the 'God who acts to save'—or more specifically, the 'God who acts mightily in history'.

In broad terms the exodus consists of an extended series of events including the plagues, the departure from Egypt, the crossing of the sea and the celebration of that crossing in song. In the study that follows, I will focus on what happens to the waters in these narratives.

As we might suspect, the plagues have been interpreted primarily as expressions of God's mighty power in liberating God's people. We readily identify with the suffering Israelites and celebrate the victory of Israel's god over the gods of Egypt.

A number of scholars have sought to retrieve the naturally occurring phenomena behind the plagues described in Exodus. For example, Greta Hort[4] espoused a theory based on the infrequent occurrence of an unusually heavy rainfall in the highlands of Ethiopia. The annual rise of the river that starts in July and reaches its peak in mid-September is said, on rare occasions, to result in catastrophe rather than fertility. The soil in the basin of the Blue Nile and its tributary, the Atbara, is red. This red sediment emerges along the Nile when floods from the highlands pour downstream and discolour the waters so that they look like blood. Similar natural explanations, based on this same flooding phenomenon, are used to explain the subsequent plagues. The text, however, is concerned with the event as a bold and destructive act of God. What really happened in natural terms is not the agenda of this grey text; it is a reconstruction of scholars.

Though the 'bloody Nile' is an ominous water event dominating the exodus narrative, the focus of scholars has been on the cry of Moses to 'let my people go'. The focus of interpreters is understandably anthropocentric and they identify with the oppressed humans, the Israelites. No one, to my knowledge, has dared to identify with the waters.

Yet the waters of the Nile are life-giving, a massive ecosystem that sustains both humans and nonhumans along the length of the Nile. The waters of the Nile are the lifeblood of several countries. The waters of

---

4. Greta Hort, 'The Plagues of Egypt', *ZAW* 69, 1957: 85–103; 70, 1958: 48–59.

the Nile flow for some 3500 miles with a watershed that is estimated to be about a million acres. The Nile, and the ancient Nile god Hapi, represent the waters of life for millions of people, plants and other living creatures in this region.

If we now dare to focus on the Nile as a living subject in the narrative, we gain a sense of injustice at what happens: the Nile is assaulted. God informs Moses that God will 'strike the water of the Nile', an act designed to impart a curse (cf Exod 7:25). The symbol of that curse is blood: the lifeblood of the land is turned into blood that is shed—bloodshed: the symbol of death. The waters of life can no longer sustain life. Instead of water, there is blood 'throughout all the land of Egypt'. The land is like a bleeding corpse.

The grey text in question reads:

> The Lord said to Moses "Say to Aaron, 'Take your staff and stretch out your hand over the waters of Egypt—over its rivers, its canals, and its ponds, and all its pools of water—so that they may become blood; there shall be blood throughout the whole land of Egypt, even in vessels of wood and in vessels of stone'."
> (Exod 7:19)

Fretheim suggests that the image of water as shed blood anticipates the sea becoming red with Egyptian blood. He argues that this image is a sign. For Fretheim, it is 'more than just a bloody mess, a lot of dead fish and a headache for waterworks personnel'[5]. Blood, a sign of deliverance for Israel (Exod 12:13) is a sign of disaster for Egypt.

I would argue, however, that this blood is also a sign of physical abuse. God striking the waters is a cruel blow that results in blood and death. God strikes the waters—not because they are explicitly in league with Pharaoh or the oppressors; they are apparently collateral damage in the war of YHWH against Pharaoh and the gods of Egypt. There is no obvious ecological interconnection between the oppressors and the waters.

Already in the plagues, we meet the demonising of the waters and related figures. Symbols of life are portrayed as symbols of death or chaos in the hyperbole of conflict. The so-called snakes that emerge from the staff of Aaron are designated *tannin*: sea monsters associated with

---

5. Terence Fretheim, 'The Reclamation of Creation: Redemption and Law in Exodus', *Interpretation* 45, 1991: 388.

watery chaos, who 'swallow' the snakes produced by the magicians. These *tannin* (Exod 7:12) anticipate the demonising of the sea which is also called *tannin* and slain by the God, the warrior, in Ps 74:13.

In his 1991 article, Fretheim sought to demonstrate that the plagues were ecological signs of historical disaster. He argued that Egypt and Pharaoh were the embodiment of the forces of chaos threatening a return of the entire cosmos to a pre-creation state[6]. While I agree that certain images of the creation tradition may well inform the language of the narrative, I would argue that the account does not reflect the effect of humans causing ecological disasters. Whatever the political sin of Pharaoh, the plagues are direct acts of God that intervene and create disasters that do not correspond to the pattern of natural ecosystems. God's actions seem to be anti-ecological hypernatural intrusions into the cosmic order. God uses the waters to force Pharaoh's hand, regardless of the consequences for the rest of creation in Egypt. What happens to the waters of the Nile is typical of what happens to other domains of nature in the plagues and throughout the exodus event.

In the Exodus narrative, YHWH's mighty acts of deliverance for Israel are at the same time mighty acts of destruction for nature.

But why should the Nile be polluted by God and all its life-giving waters turned to blood when all God had to do was change the mind of one man—Pharaoh? Why destroy millions of creatures in the Nile ecosystem? All God had to do was NOT to harden Pharaoh's heart! Why should the waters of the Nile be demonised when a human being called Pharaoh is the real demon?

When scholars do focus on the water events, they try to retrieve natural phenomena that could possibly explain the events. The waters of the Nile, however, are victims of divine pollution; they have been unfairly demonised as forces for a warrior God to conquer. These water ecosystems have been violated and their true life-giving character denied. Some may describe these water events as evidence of the sovereignty of God over nature, but clearly God's sovereignty is devoid of empathy here. There is no rainbow at the end of these water events to suggest God will never again violate nature's ecosystems.

---

6. Fretheim, 'Reclamation', 385–6.

The exodus event may well be a symbol for liberation of oppressed peoples; it is not, however, a symbol or expression of liberation for Earth or Earth's ecosystems. The texts reporting the plagues and the crossing of the Red Sea reveal these mighty acts of God as destructive deeds against innocent domains of nature.

Acts of God in Ezekiel

I have focused above on the way God destroyed Earth and Earth creatures during the flood and how God performed acts of destruction in nature to deliver Israel from slavery. References to God intervening in history with acts of punishment or liberation that caused the destruction of many parts of creation—everything from the primal flood to fleas that plagued Pharaoh—are not, however, confined to early traditions of deliverance.

According to Israel's prophets, similar divine acts of judgment are repeatedly imposed on domains of nature when God punishes Israel or another nation. The prophet Ezekiel, for example, often depicts God as bringing disaster on lands and mountains as well as peoples, thereby devaluing the natural world to facilitate God's punishing inappropriate human behaviour[7].

When YHWH destroys a nation in Ezekiel, for example, all livestock are removed along with the humans. The pattern of destruction implicating the natural world reflected in the flood account persists.

More specifically, what is removed from the landscape is its 'fullness'. Recalling the famous cry in Isaiah's vision, it is clear that the fullness is more than the land's contents (Isa 6:3). This fullness is the very life of the land. Without its fullness, the land is dead, a valley of dry bones; the land is a *terra nullius*, totally devalued.

Ezekiel's words of judgment reflect a repeated pattern of injustice and abuse against nature. On one occasion, Ezekiel is summoned to announce a fire and 'preach against the South and prophesy against the forest land in the Negeb' (Ezek 20:46). All forms of life, from both the North and the South, are summoned to watch the fire destroy the forest, their natural habitat. This is not a natural process; it is direct divine

---

7. Norman Habel, 'The Silence of the Lands: the Ecojustice Implications of Ezekiel's Judgement Oracles', in *Ezekiel's Hierarchical World—Wrestling with Tiered Reality* (Symposium 31; Atlanta: SBL, 2004), 127–40.

intervention designed to let all living creatures know that YHWH has destroyed their homes. The forest is an innocent victim.

On another occasion, Ezekiel directs his divine oracles against the mountains (Ezek 6:1–14). While the mountains may to some extent be a metonymy for the people of the land, they also represent the land that is made totally desolate (Ezek 6:14). Once again, the mountains are innocent victims. In Ezekiel, creation is viewed as expendable property[8]. Creation seems to have no intrinsic value; it can be burned or battered at will by divine acts of violence. Both Earth and the Earth community suffer unjustly as YHWH makes the landscape desolate (cf Ezek 33:23–29).

Zion, at the centre of Ezekiel's cosmos, has supreme worth because it is the chosen locus of God's sanctuary: the abode of the 'glory of God'. Jerusalem, with her dubious Canaanite origins, has no intrinsic value (Ezek 16:1–5). Jerusalem is endowed with value because of the special transformation effected by YHWH—a consequence of God selecting the city as the site for the sanctuary. Similarly, the 'land of Israel', as the settled land in which the sacred mountain is located, has no value as part of Earth. Its value is fortuitous: it is the ground on which the sanctuary is constructed. Land, as human habitation, can actually disappear and cease to exist.

> **Ezekiel is perhaps the most forceful of the prophets in his portraits of how the mighty acts of divine judgment impact on the natural world. Similar grey images persist, however, in the words of many of Israel's prophets. The question we must explore is whether there are corresponding green texts in tension with these oracles and whether the New Testament has a different orientation.**

The challenge

In the recent history of humankind there are numerous indications that nations and individuals feel justified in 'playing God' by interfering in nature with acts that destroy not only human beings but the natural environment. God as represented in these biblical texts provides

---

8. Julie Galambush, 'Castles in the Air: Creation as Property in Ezekiel' (*Ezekiel Seminar Paper*; Atlanta: SBL, 2000).

them with precedents for this callous indifference to Earth even if the provocation is allegedly another nation.

The bombing of Hiroshima and Nagasaki were horrendous acts of destruction that not only killed humans but let loose masses of radioactive energy into the atmosphere, killing life for miles around the blast site. Even the testing of nuclear weapons left vast areas of land radioactive and deadly to most forms of life for generations. The British nuclear tests at Maralinga in the centre of Australia are a case in point.

The stockpiling of nuclear weapons is an indication that nations are still ready to play God and send nuclear plagues to destroy Earth. The God of this grey text, it seems, has a lot to answer for!

There are numerous other examples of how humans have felt free to violate nature in the interests of human victory, progress or preservation. Agent Orange, used in the Vietnam war, is a good example. Not only were innocent humans subjected to cruelty and suffering: the natural environment was transformed into an unnatural landscape, devoid of vegetation and other living things. Humans imposed a plague in Vietnam much as their God had done in ancient Egypt. In our contemporary world of endemic climate change and ecological stress, the precedent set by God as depicted in this grey text can no longer be ignored.

The mighty acts of God have long been associated with YHWH as a god who delivers, redeems the people of God. But at what cost to nature? These grey texts illustrate an alternative portrait of God in the Old Testament. The flood texts and the exodus texts illustrate how the natural world is devalued by the acts of God in the interests of humans, to achieve an anthropocentric outcome. Deliverance is achieved at the expense of nature; salvation is wrought through the cruel manipulation and abusive destruction of creation.

The Old Testament God who acts in history does not appear to support the greening of creation as a priority! Are we still prone to play 'God' by emulating this understanding of God in the text?

Or is the problem that 'grey' interpreters have turned the deity of these texts into an idol, an image of God they wish to imitate rather than critique by engaging with alternative readings of these passages? I will explore an alternative reading strategy in chapter 7.

There is a small island in the Pacific Ocean called Tuvalu. This island will be one of the first to be flooded by the rise of the ocean due to global warming. I have been told that the Christian elders of this island refuse to accept this eventuality. Why? Because God will be faithful to the 'rainbow covenant' and never flood Earth again. Does the record of God's mighty acts after the flood justify their faith in this God and the promise symbolised by the rainbow?

3

The Promised Land Syndrome

'The Lord has given us this land.'
1992 memorial text

Adelaide in South Australia is known as the 'city of churches'. It acquired this title in the mid-nineteenth century, not because it erected numerous church buildings, but because it was open to any religious group who chose to settle there. Unlike the other states of Australia, South Australia was not a convict colony; it was a free settlement open to people from throughout Europe. It was another promised land.

One group of settlers was a Lutheran contingent from Germany. They appropriated land in the Barossa Valley, cleared the trees, and planted what is now one of the richest vineyards in the world. In the process they forced most of the indigenous inhabitants to leave the region.

In 1995, these immigrant Australians erected a monument on a hill high above the valley in memory of their achievements. They chose a text from the promised land tradition in the book of Joshua for their memorial: 'The Lord has given us this land' (Josh 2:10). For these settlers, the valley was indeed their promised land: a land God gave them to colonise. In the process the original inhabitants, like the Canaanites, had their land taken from them and were forced into exile.

The promised land ideology has played a major role in Christian and Jewish thinking for centuries. The meanings associated with this ideology range from hopes about a secure homeland to dreams about heaven. The promised land has been employed as a lofty theme in hymns—and as an ugly impetus for wars.

The narrative that portrays the entry of the people of ancient Israel into their promised land is located in the book of Joshua. Joshua is depicted as the hero of ancient Israel's conquest of Canaan. And the book of Joshua seems to epitomise a particular understanding of the promised land that I have designated 'the promised land syndrome'. An alternative understanding of the land is reflected in the Genesis narratives where Abraham is depicted as a guest in the land and the Canaanites as the host peoples[1].

In the context of Western colonial history and the current environmental crisis, I believe there are several grey texts promoting a promised land mindset that continue to haunt us. These texts, I would argue, are in direct conflict with a healthy ecological worldview.

The divine right of the invaders

Some years ago, in my book *The Land is Mine,* I identified six biblical land ideologies. In the book of Joshua, I identified an ancestral household ideology according to which the land is divided into family lots[2].

The stories about the allotment and taking possession of the allotments in Joshua 13–21 are framed by conquest narratives (Joshua 1–12) and closing speeches ascribed to Joshua (Joshua 23–24). Integral to this framework are bold statements that all of YHWH's 'promises' made to the ancestors had been kept as Moses predicted. Admittedly, this version of the conquest probably does not correspond to known history; as an ideology, however, it has influenced subsequent events in history. Moreover, the portrait of the Canaanites in Joshua is likely to reflect the writer's promised land ideology rather than an understanding of the true identity of the inhabitants of the land[3].

The promise of land that God swore to the ancestors is cited in Joshua as a charter which justifies the invasion of land, the conquest of the Canaanites, and the allocation of the land of Canaan to families. The granting and allocation of land seems to be portrayed as a legal grant of property[4]. The Joshua narrative grounds ancient Israel's claim to land— both in terms of divine right and legal authority

How is this divine right interpreted? After visiting Rahab, a Canaanite who saves them from capture, the spies announce what amounts to a divine verdict on the situation: 'Truly YHWH has given all the land into your hands' (Josh 2:24). In other words, the narrator claims that ancient

---

1. Norman Habel, *The Land Is Mine. Six Biblical Land Ideologies* (Minneapolis: Fortress, 1995), chapter 7.

2. Habel, *Land Ideologies,* chapter 4.

3. Niels Peter Lemche, *The Canaanites and Their Land. The Tradition of the Canaanites* (JSOT Supplement Series 110; Sheffield: JSOT Press, 1991), 165.

4. Harry Orlinsky, 'The Biblical Concept of the Land of Israel: Cornerstone of the Covenant between God and Israel', in LA Hoffman, ed, *The Land of Israel: Jewish Perspectives* (Notre Dame: University of Notre Dame Press, 1986), 27–64.

Israel have a divine right to possess the land as a grant. Evidence of this forthcoming possession is that the inhabitants have been transformed into weaklings 'melting with fear'.

This word of God from the mouth of spies is a prelude to the invasion of Canaan. After celebrating the Passover in their newly acquired land, the manna from heaven ceases and the invaders survive by eating the crops of Canaan, a sign that God is now meeting their needs with blessings from the land.

> **Ancient Israel's divine right to the promised land is also interpreted as a right to conquer, kill and destroy. In fact, this process goes so far as to 'devote to YHWH by destroying' (*cherem* in Hebrew).**

Destroying all cities, human lives and livestock is viewed by the narrator as a mandate from YHWH to dedicate the conquest of the promised land to YHWH, in effect, a 'massive holocaust offering'. The land is apparently all that remains after YHWH has been satisfied with destruction in YHWH's name. Anyone who dares to defy this mandate—like Achan— is burned alive.

The *modus operandi* of Joshua as God's agent in the conquest of Canaan seems to model the way in which YHWH employed destructive acts against humanity and nature to deliver Israel from Egypt. The blessing in the form of the land grant, which follows their deliverance from slavery, is effected by treating any life other than that of the chosen people as fair game, and destined for destruction. From an ecological perspective, these are indeed grey texts.

This divine right to massacre the human inhabitants even seems to have cosmic support: when Joshua fights the kings of the Amorites, YHWH rains down stones from heaven to help the invading army to victory. And when daytime runs out before they can complete the killing, Joshua has the sun stand still in the sky until the deed is done (Josh 10:11–13). At the head of the invading army is the ominous figure of YHWH, the warrior God who makes sure the devastation is total. All of nature, it seems, is at God's deadly disposal in a holy war of conquest.

The outcome of Joshua's campaigns is summarised as a total conquest that corresponds to God's promise. Joshua takes 'the whole land according to what the Lord has spoken to Moses' (Josh 11:23). The

promised land is the land God promised to assign to Joshua's people, a
gift delivered through conquest, destruction and killing.

> **The promised land in the book of Joshua is not only a land
> flowing with milk and honey but with blood and brutality.**

If we are being honest, we will acknowledge that in the history of
interpretation, the book of Joshua has provided a charter for a promised
land syndrome—a pattern of behaviour at various points in history
which has been invoked to justify the conquest and killing of inhabitants
of other lands as a divine right. Various Christian interpreters and
colonial leaders have used this promised land tradition as a justification
for conquests of peoples and the destruction of ecosystems.

Rights of the inhabitants of the land

Deuteronomy begins with Moses and the Israelites leaving Mt Horeb to
travel across the wilderness to take possession of the land promised to
their ancestors, Abraham, Isaac and Jacob. The expectation, announced
to the Israelites by Moses, is that YHWH their God will clear away all
the inhabitants so that the Israelites can 'utterly destroy' them and avoid
any chance of a covenant with the inhabitants (Deut 7:1–2). For Israel to
multiply and enjoy the many blessings of the promised land, however,
they must obey the laws of Moses (Deut 6:1–3). In order to effect the
conquest of the promised land, they are expected to follow the rules of
holy war: destroy all humans and livestock—everything except the fruit
trees (Deuteronomy 20).

From the perspective of the ancient Canaanites—the existing
inhabitants of the land—the invaders' promised land policy recorded in
Joshua is unjust and cruel. The Canaanites have been the custodians of
the land for centuries, developing local forms of agriculture and animal
husbandry. Even though the ancient Israelites first consume the existing
produce of the land, the contribution of the Canaanite farmers is ignored
(Josh 5:12). In the Joshua version of the entry into Canaan, the land is
a grant from YHWH, and the indigenous inhabitants are extended no
rights or recognition.

The unjust character of the conquest as recorded in Joshua is highlighted
by the fact that the invading people do not offer to make a treaty or
covenant with the Canaanites. The precedent of the covenant Abraham

makes with Abimelech, found in Gen 21:23, seems to be a tradition that has been conveniently forgotten by the time of the conquest.

The Abraham narratives in Genesis provide a radical alternative to the promised land syndrome of Joshua. These narratives reflect an ideology of the land as a host country where Abraham is an immigrant[5]. In this text, the Canaanites and their guests, the family of Abraham, coexist: peaceful relations are established through a covenant with the hosts. From the perspective of these host peoples in the Genesis account, Joshua's destruction of the Canaanites is not only a breach of covenant; it is a violation of the covenant goodwill that gave the Abrahamic peoples access to the land of Canaan in the first place.

> **The promised land syndrome derived from Joshua conveniently ignores the goodness and generosity of the host peoples and the model of covenant justice for the land espoused by the covenant between Abimelech and Abraham.**

Promised land campaigns

This promised land syndrome has influenced the conquest of many indigenous peoples and the exploitation of their lands. Australia's Aboriginal peoples, for example, were said to no longer be *imago dei*, in the image of God. They were perceived to be like animals who, as a consequence, could be hunted down and destroyed with impunity.

Harris asserts:

> it was not simply that 'like the Hittites, and the Jebusites and the Aboriginal Canaanites, they had been left to the natural consequences of not retaining the knowledge of God' but that of all people in that condition, the Aborigines were judged to be on 'the lowest scale of degraded humanity'[6].

A Sydney barrister expressed a common attitude in *The Colonist* newspaper in 1838 when he claimed that Aborigines had 'no right to the land' because 'it belonged to him who first cultivated it'.

---

5. Habel, *Land Ideologies*, chapter 7.
6. John Harris, *One Blood: 200 Years of Aboriginal Encounter with Christianity; a Story of Hope* (Sydney: Albatross Books, 1990), 30.

Michael Prior, who traces the history of colonial invasion in South Africa and South America, poses the question of what happens when we read the text from the perspective of the original inhabitants of the promised land[7]. The invasion of South Africa by the Boers was driven by the same syndrome. As they trekked, the Boers considered themselves to be the chosen people, rescued from their 'Egypt'—British oppression— on their way to the promised land[8].

In recent times, the promised land syndrome has, in the mind of British rulers, also provided the justification for the formation of the state of Israel and the subsequent viewing of the existing inhabitants as a lesser people. Mitri Raheb, a leading voice for peace in Palestine, was invited to deliver the Charles Strong Trust lecture in Adelaide in July 2006, but was not granted a visa to come to Australia. In the lecture, which I delivered on his behalf, he writes about the colonial orientation of British politics at the time, and the way a promised land ideology derived from Joshua guided their thinking.

> What is obvious here in this theology is the ease with which Lord Earl Shaftesbury moved between biblical prophecies and British national politics. England was here seen as the instrument for fulfilling the Divine plan.
>
> The cynical aspect of the liberal theology is, however, that precisely those theologians who tried to counteract the spiritualization of Judaism (into a religion) and of the promise of land (into eternal life), either knowingly or unknowingly, fell into the trap of spiritualizing the land in another way. They referred to the land—or more specifically 'the land of Palestine'—as if it were an unpopulated space (*terra nullius*), that had remained a fallow land, and as if there were no people with a two-thousand-year history who had continued to live on this land[9].

---

7. Michael Prior, *The Bible and Colonialism: a Moral Critique.* (Sheffield: Sheffield Academic Press, 1997), 43.

8. Michael Prior, *Bible and Colonialism*, 81.

9. Mitri Raheb, 'Land, People and Identities: a Palestinian Perspective' (*2006 Charles Strong Trust Lecture; s*ee www.charlesstrongtrust .org.au/lectures).

This reference suggests that the juxtaposition of the promised land syndrome and the *terra nullius* claim persisted well into the twentieth century. The land of Palestine, like other colonised lands such as Australia, were declared to be *terra nullius*: lands with no inhabitants, or more precisely, no legal inhabitants. The indigenous inhabitants of these colonised lands, as was the case with the ancient Canaanites, were reduced to non-entities whose elimination is deemed to be acceptable in God's eyes. Invaders, therefore, claimed to have a legal right to invade the land.

Walter Brueggemann, in the preface to his second edition of *The Land*[10] recognises

> that the claim of 'promised land' in the Old Testament is not an innocent theological claim, but is a vigorous ideological assertion on an important political scale... Israel's text proceeds on the basis of the primal promises of Genesis 12–36 to assume entitlement to the land without regard to any other inhabitants including those who may have been there prior to Israel's emergence.

> **From the perspective of the prior inhabitants of Canaan and similar countries, this promised land ideology is not only unjust and demeaning; it also dehumanises the very people who had a close bond with the land prior to invasion. Their care and concern for the land over centuries is dismissed as worthless.**

The forgotten right of the land

From the perspective of the invading people, the promised land syndrome derived from the book of Joshua provides a divine charter for invasion, destruction and annihilation. From the perspective of the inhabitants of the land, this promised land syndrome abuses their rights as fellow humans, and totally suppresses alternative traditions about their future in the land. The rights of the land itself are also totally ignored.

The discussion of the promised land syndrome given above demonstrates that the text of Deuteronomy and Joshua 1–12 can be read as unequivocally anthropocentric and ethnocentric: the interests and voice of one human ethnic group are understood as having a divine

---

10. Walter Brueggemann, *The Land* (Philadelphia: Fortress Press, 2002), xiii–xiv.

right. One ethnic group is viewed as superior to another and therefore justified in conquering both the peoples and their lands. The mandate for humans to dominate Earth found in Gens 1:26–28 is translated here into a specific ideology for one ethnic group to dominate a specific land.

It is not insignificant that the explicit term for 'subduing' the land in Gen 1:28 is also employed in Josh 18:1. After subjecting the land to the *cherem*—a destructive act of devotion to YHWH—'the land lay *subdued* before them'.

> **The land is officially 'subdued' at the hands of Joshua by employing a process of destruction that demonstrates the ugly implications of the mandate to dominate. The rights and voice of the land are ignored.**

Even in the allotment of pieces of land to specific households depicted in Joshua 13–21, the land is treated as territory owned by a given 'house' in perpetuity. There is no consideration of care for the land, kinship with the land, or the goodness of the land as a precious creation of God.

The more closely we read the text, the more we get a sense that the land is victimised. With the destruction of Jericho, 'oxen, sheep and donkeys' are all destroyed as an act of devotion to God (Jos 6:21). Gold, silver and iron, however, are preserved because they are 'sacred to the Lord'. In descriptions of later conquests, the livestock of a given city are rescued: not because they are valued forms of life, but because they are 'booty' (Jos 8:27). In short, the land and living creatures of the land are not valued for themselves and their rights are ignored in these conquest narratives.

The new promised land

Images of a new promised land appear throughout the books of those prophets who anticipate Israel's return from exile, or who foresee a glorious future for the battered land of Israel—especially her sacred city Jerusalem. Some of these visions are bold and radical. According to the visions of Isaiah 65, for example, God promises that 'I am about to create new heavens and a new earth' (Isa 65:17). The use of the verb 'create' found earlier in Genesis 1, seems to suggest that this event will be comparable to the initial creation of heaven and Earth. That suggestion has led interpreters to link this vision in Isaiah with the dissolution of heaven and Earth in 2 Peter 3:10, and with the vision of a new heaven and a new Earth in the Apocalypse of John (Rev 21:1).

The vision of Isaiah 65, however, is concerned with the transformation of nature not its dissolution. The focus, as with Ezekiel, is on recreating Jerusalem so that it embraces dimensions of existence beyond life as it has been known. There will be no infant mortality; humans who are a hundred years old will be considered young. The inhabitants of the city will never experience the frustration of not enjoying the labour of their hands.

One of the famous images of this transformed land is that of the earlier messianic dream (Isa 11:6–9) where the wolf and the lamb feed together, the lion eats straw like the ox, and no creature ever hurts another creature (Isa 65:25). In short, the food chain and the ecosystem as we know it is no longer valued. Visions of the future Jerusalem in Isaiah and elsewhere depict a domain that anticipates the 'new Jerusalem'. God transforms nature as we know it, thereby implying, it would seem, that our present natural world is inferior and will be replaced by a 'new promised land', and a glorious 'new city' called Jerusalem.

These visions of the new heaven and new Earth seem to anticipate God's transformation or recreation of nature, and eliminating many of the domains and ecosystems that are vital to life as we know it. These texts have led many readers, I would argue, to anticipate a heaven-like world that will render this present world obsolete. In these grey texts, the present ecosystem is not valued, preserved or restored. In these grey texts God is not happy to dwell in creation as created; God intervenes from the outside, transforms creation and includes celestial or non-natural domains.

As a consequence, some Christians view the present world and universe as transitory and of less importance than the future universe, the promised land that descends from above. Earth is devalued in the popular mind because these grey texts of the Bible promise a transformed cosmos somewhere in the future. As Denis Edwards[11] notes:

> If Christianity is understood to be about leaving this world
> for a heavenly world, if we are only on this world for a
> short time before abandoning it for another, more spiritual
> one, then this world is devalued. It is merely a step along

---

11. Denis Edwards, *Ecology at the Heart of Faith; the Change of Heart that Leads to a New Way of Living on Earth* (New York: Orbis, 2006), 82.

the way to something that is our ultimate goal. Some
Christians think this way, and as a result, even when they
value non-human creation as a gift of God, it has no final
meaning. It is left behind on the spiritual journey to a better
world.

> **This perspective may well be designated 'heavenism'. In popular
> terms it means: we believers are going to heaven so to hell with
> Earth!**

The reason why many Christians may think this way—and thereby
devalue the planet of this world—is the array of texts which depict the
transformed 'new world' using vivid and appealing imagery. These
readings from this inconvenient text called the Bible have contributed
to the devaluation of our planet home in favour of a celestial abode—
whether we like it nor not

The challenge

The ideology of the promised land syndrome views land as a possession
through conquest rather than as promise: the gift of community. Creation
is there to be colonised! The land that in Genesis was believed to 'flow
with milk and honey', the land that sustained both the Canaanites and
the family of Abraham, the land that was the locus for God's blessing, is
viewed in the book of Joshua as a land that can be exploited and owned,
a land in which God fights a holy war of conquest and destruction.

The promised land in many biblical texts is not depicted as a green and
bountiful blessing, but as a piece of property to be conquered, subdued
and exploited. In these grey texts the interests of the land and its original
inhabitants are ignored in favour of the interests of the invading people.
The promised land may be perceived as a divine gift, but at what cost to
the land itself? The gift of the promised land is a reality that some people
enjoy, but not one that the land itself relishes.

The promised land tradition also plays a role in prophetic and
apocalyptic visions of the future. Once again, the land's natural
ecosystems are devalued in favour of a transformation that a select
number of human inhabitants will celebrate and enjoy: wilderness
becomes a garden for faithful humans; the new Jerusalem is a more
fertile garden than Earth as we know it. The challenge before us is to ask
whether any of the promised land texts are anything other than grey.

Do any promised land texts reflect an ideology where the interests of a chosen human group does not outweigh any concern for the preservation of Earth and the Earth community in its natural state?

4

The Challenge of Ecology

*'In the middle of all sits the sun on his throne,
as upon a royal dais ruling his children, the planets who circle him.'*
Copernicus, De Revolutionibus

In a quiet bay on Kangaroo Island, on the Southern shores of Australia, there is a monument to Nicholas Baudin, noted French scientist and explorer. He circumnavigated the planet in 1802 and docked for a brief stay on an island replete with distinctive fauna and flora that fascinated the Frenchman. Later he met the English explorer Matthew Flinders in Encounter Bay and shared his findings, even though France and England were at war at the time. The natural world meant more to them than the politics of Europe.

Circumnavigating the globe was possible because of a radical change in the way people viewed their relationship with Earth. Their geocentric cosmology or Earth-centred view of the universe had been a long-held constant until the discoveries of Galileo and Copernicus transformed the way humans perceived their world. Copernicus, following the lead of earlier thinkers, maintained a heliocentric theory of the universe: the sun sits in the centre of the universe ruling his children, the planets. In the seventeenth century, Galileo, who promoted the theory of Copernicus, developed the first map of Earth as a globe. He was forced to face the Inquisition and was imprisoned for his writings. By the eighteenth century, however, it was accepted that ships could sail around the circumference of planet Earth and explore its grand diversity of life.

In the centuries before these discoveries, Earth was considered to be the centre of the universe. Accepted as scientific truth, the texts of Genesis depicted a primitive cosmology that represented the predominant view: the sky is a solid canopy with waters above it and Earth is an island with waters surrounding it. The so-called 'flat Earth' worldview was the prevailing view until scientists could demonstrate that Earth was round and humans could circumnavigate it.

In the words of McDonagh[1],

> While this new Copernican theory opened up the immense
> universe for observation, and gave a more adequate
> explanation for the movement of heavenly bodies, it came
> as a profound shock to many people. The dethronement of
> the Earth from the centre of creation was seen as a challenge
> both to Ptolemaic astronomy and, more important still, to
> orthodox theology.

Our understanding of the cosmos has changed considerably since the days
of Copernicus and Galileo. We are faced with another profound shock:
theories of evolution, astrophysics and genetics have all contributed to a
new appreciation of the planet as a vibrant speck of stardust in an almost
endless cosmos. We have reached a point where suggestions of a seven-
day creation seem ludicrous even to faithful Christians. The biblical texts
can no longer be read literally in the light of current evidence as to the
age and formation of our planet.

What has emerged, I would argue, is a new view of the natural world
that scholars have defined in various ways. A crucial dimension of this
emerging worldview is 'ecology'. And the challenge before us today is
no less than it was for those who faced the Copernican revolution.

**We are faced with the Bible being an inconvenient text—and the
challenge to read that text in the context of an emerging view of
the natural world.**

Ecological conversion

In his January 2001 general audience address, Pope John Paul II introduced
a new idea: the need for an *ecological conversion*. Catholic theologians
such as Denis Edwards have promoted this concept as integral to the
development of ecotheology[2]. The context of this concept is the growing
ecological crisis and our emerging awareness of its implications. The
dilemma before us concerns our Christian understanding of this laudable
idea: from what are we being converted; to what are we being converted?

---

1. Sean McDonagh, *To Care for the Earth. A Call to a New Theology* (London: Geoffrey
   Chapman, 1986), 62.
2. Edwards, *Heart of Faith*, 2–4.

What are the parameters of this 'conversion' experience?

In the words of Edwards[3],

> Commitment to ecology has not yet taken its central place in Christian self-understanding. It is far from central in terms of its structure, personnel and money. As the church itself is called to conversion to the side of the poor in the struggle of justice and to the side of women in their struggle for full equality, so the church itself is called to conversion to the side of suffering creation.

If this conversion means taking a stand at the side of suffering creation, joining the struggle for ecojustice and seeking to heal the wounds of our planet, the process is indeed worthy and vital. In this context, the question at hand is: what does an ecological conversion mean for the way we read the Bible? Edwards' term 'suffering creation' presumably relates to the current ecological crisis. How does this Christ-centred ecological awareness influence our interpretation of earlier biblical traditions and ways of reading that have contributed to the suffering of creation?

Another way of addressing this challenge is to speak of 'greening' our world and our way of thinking. In the past, 'greening' has been viewed as a rather trite popular term for 'those eccentrics' in the ecological movement: 'greenies'. The term 'green', however, has come of age and is now employed to identify the orientation of those seeking to integrate ecology with a range of fields of thought and action. As I noted earlier, to be green is to empathise with nature.

One Christian ecological movement, The Green Seminary Initiative, seeks to promote the care of creation as an integral part of seminary education[4]; their goal: every seminarian, and ultimately every church served by that seminarian, will learn the scriptural, theological, historical and spiritual foundations of Earth-care. The courses at the seminary are designed to integrate ecology with every aspect of life and learning, thereby greening everything from worship to ethics and from policies to politics. The question still remains: what do ecology and green mean in the context of biblical studies?

The *Green Seminary Policy Statement* advocates that 'We accept our vocation as earth-keepers who care for creation. We see ourselves as

---

3. Edwards, *Heart of Faith*, 3.
4. See www.webofcreation.org/GreenSeminary.

part of the covenant of Noah that God made with humans and with all animals of the land, sea and air.' Given our earlier discussion of the way God is portrayed in the grey text that relates the Noah covenant, the challenge becomes: what does green mean in connection with biblical studies—does greening mean the selection of convenient texts that support Earth-care, or does it also require a critical re-appraisal of the inconvenient grey texts?

If, as I have demonstrated, the Bible is not necessarily green, what does it mean to integrate ecology and biblical studies? What does the greening of biblical studies ultimately mean?

In a somewhat different vein, Thomas Berry speaks of the 'great work'[5] that we are summoned to undertake as we move

> the human project from its devastating exploitation to a benign presence...Our own special role, which we will hand on to our children, is that of managing the arduous transition from the terminal Cenozoic to the emerging Ecozoic era, the period where humans will be present to the planet as participating members of the comprehensive Earth community.

Berry compares the radical change demanded for us to undertake this work with that of the emergence of Western civilisation in the thirteenth century. This work demands a basic transformation of our relationship with this planet and a bold assessment of the traditions we have inherited that justify our current patterns of exploitation at the hands of human technology. And whether we like it or not, the biblical heritage is one of those traditions. As we proceed with this 'great work' of integrating our being into the ecosystems of Earth, what do we do with the biblical texts that tend to alienate us from Earth rather than consciously integrate our being into the Earth community?

---

5. Thomas Berry, *The Great Work. Our Way into the Future* (New York: Bell Tower, 1999), 7.

An ecology-informed worldview

As ecological Christians, we are faced, it seems to me, with the challenge of a new view of the natural world, a new understanding of the universe, a new cosmology that has little in common with the biblical, geocentric or heliocentric cosmologies of the past. Our challenge: to embrace an eco-cosmology, a worldview where ecology conditions our thinking.

What is ecology? According to the *Oxford Dictionary of Ecology*, ecology is 'the scientific study of the interrelationships among organisms and between them and all aspects, living and non-living, of their environment'[6].

This definition reflects a very limited perspective which locates ecology as one scientific discipline among many. In reality, ecology has now become an integral part of our social, political and personal worlds. And if we are to face the challenge of ecology in biblical studies we need to articulate what ecology really means as part of our emerging ecology-oriented worldview.

Another somewhat broader definition, found in the popular work *Your Eco Handbook*[7]: ecology is the 'science concerned with the macro and the micro study of the biosphere, its systems, and the relationships between organisms and between organisms and their environment'.

Most of the scholars who explore ecotheology, ecoethics and similar fields rarely begin by defining just what they mean by 'ecology' or 'green'. They often take the meaning of these terms for granted.

How might we describe the understanding of ecology that informs an ecology-oriented worldview? One option is the formulation of Thomas Berry[8]:

> In reality there is a single integral community of the Earth that includes all its component members whether human or other than human. In this community every being has its own role to fulfil, its own dignity, its inner spontaneity. Every being has its own voice. Every being declares itself to the entire universe. Every being enters into communion

---

6. Michael Allaby, *A Dictionary of Ecology* (2nd edn; Oxford: Oxford University Press, 1998), 136.
7. Grahame Barrett et al, *Your Eco Handbook. Achieving a Sustainable Future* (Sydney: Fairfax Books, 2007), 111.
8. Berry, *Great work*, 4.

with other beings. This capacity for relatedness, for presence
to other beings, for spontaneity in action, is a capacity
possessed by every mode of being throughout the entire
universe. So too every being has rights to be recognised
and revered.

Another option, from Sallie McFague[9]:

> The study of ecology is the most basic knowledge that
> we need to help us make the shift to a new way of seeing
> ourselves. Ecology is, at its simplest, 'words about
> home': *oikos* (home) and *logos* (word). Ecology is not an
> esoteric subject reserved for experts, but information
> about planet Earth—its nature and its rules, and hence
> where we fit into it. Ecology is a study that we should
> begin in infancy and continue through adulthood. If we
> are to turn away from anthropocentrism—the focus on
> ourselves as masters of the earth—to cosmocentrism—
> the focus on the earth and where we belong in it—we
> need a **functional** creation story.

Combining these understandings of Thomas Berry and Sallie McFague
with the ecojustice principles enunciated several years ago as part of *The
Earth Bible* project[10], I believe it is possible to outline key dimensions of an
emerging worldview informed by ecology. In outlining this worldview,
however, I will also take into account certain broader cultural perceptions
that characterise contemporary thinking about our world.

In our current cosmology or ecology informed view of the natural
world—and more particularly of Earth—I would suggest that we accept
the following as basic tenets:

---

9. Sallie McFague, *A New Climate for Theology. God, the World and Global Warming*
    (Minneapolis: Fortress, 2008), 48–9.
10. Habel, 'Geophany', 34–48.

> Earth is a planet that originated in cosmic space and evolved into a living habitat.
>
> Earth is a fragile web of interconnected and interdependent forces and domains of existence.
>
> Earth is a living community in which humans and all other organisms are kin who live and move and have their common destiny.

Earth as living planet

For many people in the twenty-first century, Earth is no longer simply a planet that orbits the sun and provides sustenance for human beings. Earth is located in the Milky Way, a small galaxy in the vastness of interstellar space. Earth is a piece of blue–green stardust that we have only recently been able to view as a whole planet—through the lens of a camera out in space. Earth is a magic moment in a massive schema of cosmic time!

We are also becoming increasingly aware that this planet called Earth is unique within the few realms of the cosmos that we have been able to explore to date. A television show in 2007, 'The birth of Earth,' reconstructed the origins of our planet as a living habitat: the stages of its evolution, including the creation of water; the origin of oxygen; and the generation of life. We now understand that Earth is an amazing and precious planet, full of ecological mysteries yet to be appreciated or understood.

We are also more conscious of Earth as a living planet. All of its components, from the mountains to the forests, from the oceans to the Antarctic, are part of a complex living entity. And we humans—along with all other living beings—are a privileged integral part of this living planet Earth. And not only is Earth a unique living planet in our galaxy: Earth provides the habitat which nurtures all consciousness as we know it. We no longer dwell 'on Earth' we live 'in Earth.'

> Earth is a living home to be revered, loved and celebrated.

Earth as fragile web

Perhaps the contemporary force that has been most influential in changing our worldview has been the environmental crisis. We have become acutely aware that Earth is not a collection of separate continents or bodies of land separated by waters, or discrete domains isolated by geographical or geological barriers. We now realise that Earth is a single domain: all its components are connected like a wondrous web. What happens in the ocean currents in one region influences life on distant shores. What happens in a desert storm influences life in rain forests.

The environmental crisis, however, has made us realise that this web of creation called planet Earth is also very fragile. And human beings, it seems, have the capacity to upset the balance of forces and impulses that govern the life of the planet. The large-scale removal of forest trees wounds the lungs of the planet. Excessive use of fossil fuels has lead to global warming across the entire globe. Planet Earth is suffering at the hands of greedy humans.

We have also come to realise that human beings are not separate or disconnected from the various forces and domains of nature. We are totally dependent on the various ecosystems of Earth for survival; these ecosystems that have existed for millennia. The movement of oxygen in the atmosphere is necessary for us to breathe. The movement of moisture in the clouds and the seas is essential for us to enjoy a drink. The movement of worms in the soil is vital for us to receive our daily bread.

Macy effectively expresses the reality that we are Earth[11]:

> Matter is made from rock and soil. It, too, is pulled by the moon as the magma circulates through the planet heart and roots such molecules into biology. Earth pours through us, replacing each cell in the body every seven years. Ashes to ashes, dust to dust, we ingest, incorporate and excrete the earth, are made from earth. I am that. You are that.

Living on this fragile planet, all creatures may face fierce and violent moments. Everything—from trees to tigers—suffers when hit by a tornado, a hurricane, an earthquake or a tsunami. The ecosystems of Earth react to various forces from outside and beyond as well as from within the planet. This planet is a volatile living body in which all life must find its place.

---

11. Joanna Macy & John Seed, 'Gaia Meditations', in Roger S Gottlieb, ed, *This Sacred Earth: Religion, Nature, Environment* (New York: Routledge, 1996), 501.

Earth is a delicate lifeline; if we want to survive with the planet
we must remain connected.

Earth as community

Recent research in the fields of biology, genetics and evolutionary
science has reminded us that we are kin with all other living things on
Earth. Human beings are related to all living things: some creatures are
close relatives and others are distant kin; some are friendly and others
are fierce. We are related to all living things: ants, elephants, sea horses,
invisible organisms... Our genetic coding differs only slightly from that
of other animals. We belong to the same family; we are a community of
kin.

Human kinship with nonhuman living creatures and the domains of
nature is something that many indigenous people know and experience.
The Australian Aborigines, for example, experience a close kinship with
nature and recognise they have a special kinship with their personal
dreaming—a bird, animal or some other life form that is part of their
everyday world. They are conscious of a common spirit in themselves,
their dreamings and the sacred sites where their dreaming ancestors
reside. Can a renewed sense of our integral kinship with nature emerge
again in our secular urban world?

Thomas Berry maintains that there is a capacity in all beings to enter into
communion with other beings[12]. Living things are not only biologically
related; they also possess an inner impulse to commune with the other
beings and to relate to the rest of the universe. The research of Ursula
Goodenough and other contemporary scholars illustrates that there are
numerous modes of communication, awareness and communion among
the members of Earth's family[13].

This community, however, is not to be idealised as 'one big happy
family' in which we enjoy the harmonious ecosystem of Eden. The
kingdoms that have evolved in the wild include carnivores that consume
herbivores and mammals that fight tooth and nail to defend their
territory. The lion does not lie down with the lamb. The fittest and the
smartest have found diverse ways of survival. Yet all of these competing

---

12. Berry, *Great work*, 4.
13. Ursula Goodenough, *The Sacred Depths of Nature* (Oxford: Oxford University
Press, 1998).

and compatible creatures are our kin, nurtured by Earth and born of its elements.

> **If we wish to have a common destiny with our kin—whatever their locus in the web of creation—we need to respect their rights and help protect their domains within this diverse interconnected ecosystem we call Earth.**

Grey texts and our new worldview

Given this portrait of our natural world informed by ecology, we are faced with a formidable challenge in relation to the grey texts I analysed in the first three chapters. I will now compare, briefly, various elements of the ecological orientation some of us have come to recognise as integral to our current worldview with the mandate to dominate analysed in chapters 1–3.

The three key features of this contemporary worldview not only challenge the basic cosmology of Genesis 1, but also the specifics of the mandate to dominate in Gen 1:26–28. Our concept of Earth as a planet originating in space and transformed into a *precious living habitat* to be revered, represents a perspective that is diametrically opposed to the directive for humans to 'subdue Earth'. The mandate to 'subdue' rather than 'revere' Earth, to 'conquer' rather than 'sustain' Earth, violates the very purpose of our human relationship with our planet home.

In many grey texts, God is represented as not being concerned about the domains of Earth as precious realms to be preserved. The destruction of lands and lives to effect the deliverance of a select group of humans— as in the plagues of Egypt—or to inflict judgments that destroy realms of nature in order to vindicate God's name, are presented as more important to God in these texts. God is even willing to go to the extent of destroying all of Earth with a flood although Earth is an innocent partner in these inconvenient texts. The God of Israel depicted in many texts of the Old Testament is willing to 'subdue' Earth in order to deliver a chosen people; the preservation of the domains of nature is secondary in many of these texts.

Our awareness that *Earth is a fragile web* of interconnected domains of existence is a vital development in a worldview influenced by and concerned about environmental disasters. We have come to realise that the various domains of nature are not disconnected, but interdependent. The mandate to dominate in Gen 1:26–28 poses a problem for an eco-cosmology: this text re-enforces a sense of disconnection between humans and the rest of nature.

In Genesis 1, humans do not emerge from the natural world; unlike the other living creatures, they are depicted as separate, distinct, and God-like. They are connected to God not to nature. As creatures bearing the image of God, human beings are given the right to dominate the rest of creation; they are not given an invitation to serve and sustain creation.

Our growing consciousness that *Earth is a community* of kin is another important element in our ecological worldview. Humans are part of the evolution of Earth into a community of interconnected beings with a common destiny.

The text of Gen 1:26–28, however, calls for humans to dominate all other living creatures, ruling over them as powerful kings. There is no sense of kinship or communion between humans and nature in this text. God places humans above nature, all creatures and Earth.

We might be tempted to view the image of Noah, his family and representative living creatures on a boat in the flood narrative as a new beginning. All the survivors are one family, a community of kin, in spite of the ugly destructive acts of God in causing the flood. We are soon disillusioned, however: the mandate to dominate is reimposed and the animal world is destined to live in fear of humanity (Gen 9:1–2). Once again nonhumans are 'delivered into the hand' of humans, their masters.

Climate change and global warming

One particular environmental crisis that is challenging our human-centred worldview is global warming and corresponding climate changes. Al Gore's film *An Inconvenient Truth* provides vivid images of the impact of these phenomena: mountains are losing their snow caps, huge bodies of polar ice are melting, portions of the planet are becoming arid and oceans are getting warmer. We have become aware that the emissions resulting from our use of fossil fuels affects the climate of the whole globe.

The anticipated effects of global warming are frightening. The loss of Greenland ice alone, if it proceeds at the current rate, will cause sea levels to rise by half a metre this century; as a consequence, many of the world's major cities will be flooded. Low lying islands will be swamped, millions of people displaced, habitats destroyed and species will disappear. Especially problematic is a temperature rise that will mean fewer acres for grain production. Already there are food shortages resulting in malnutrition and starvation in very poor countries. Food riots are a regular occurrence in parts of Africa[14].

Even more frightening is that temperatures are continuing to rise and emissions of greenhouse gases persist. More and more greenhouse gases are accumulating in Earth's atmosphere—and will remain for many hundreds of years. We are entering a new age, a greenhouse age, in which the ecosystems of Earth will have to adapt to the new gases in her lungs. And Lovelock[15] reminds us that the

> few things we do know about the response of the Earth to our presence are deeply disturbing. Even if we stopped immediately all seizing of Gaia's land and water for food and fuel production and stopped poisoning the air, it would take Earth more than a thousand years to recover from the damage we have done.

It is not only that we have a changing worldview; we also have a changing world. We will need to adapt to life in a greenhouse environment in a way we never envisaged. Climate change will not go away; Earth will respond with new ecosystems. And we will be wondering whether any of the grey texts we cited in the past are at all relevant in a greenhouse habitat.

The challenge

The time has come, I believe, to recognise that we must now read the Bible in a radically new way. We are informed by a worldview that reflects the influence of ecology as well as the current environmental crisis. While the preceding outline of that worldview is limited in this study, the three features that I have outlined are crucial: *Earth is a precious living habitat, a fragile web of ecosystems and a community of kin.* These features represent a perspective on our planet that we can no longer ignore as we read the relevant texts of Scripture. Given this perspective, there are many grey texts that are decidedly problematic.

---

14. Jonathan Boston, 'Tackling Global Warming—Now or Never', in *Tui Motu InterIslands* 55, June 2008: 14.
15. James Lovelock, *The Revenge of Gaia* (London: Allen Lane, 2006), 6.

If there is to be an 'ecological conversion', then it must also involve the question of how we interpret such texts! If there is to be a green reading, we must read with a genuine empathy for Earth as a precious planet, a fragile habitat and a living community being transformed by global warming. We humans need to read as children of Earth rather than as lords over Earth.

In Eastern Australia there is a massive river system known as the Murray–Darling Basin. It is comparable to the Missouri–Mississippi system in the USA. In the past ten years, however, not one drop of water from this Australian system has reached the ocean! Such an example should shock us into recognising that the waters of Earth are not just a source of revenue, but an integral part of who we are—whether we work, play or just read the text!

5

A Green Reading of Grey Texts

'Let the skies be glad and Earth rejoice'
Psalm 96:11

When my brother and I were boys on the farm, we learned to read the landscape and interpret the voices we heard in the bush. We could tell the next day's weather from signs in the sky. We could distinguish between a mating call and a warning cry among the birds overhead. We knew whether the roar of a bull meant he was about to charge us or if it was merely to notify us of his presence.

One sound that sometimes annoyed us was the laugh of the kookaburra. When we bicycled down to the creek at dawn to catch eels, we would hear the kookaburra laugh as the sun rose. We thought it was laughing at us—especially when we were not catching any eels! Our reading was anthropocentric: we thought its laugh must be directed at us.

How wrong we were. Years later I discovered that the kookaburra was a symbol of good news for the Indigenous peoples of Queensland in Northern Australia. The laugh of the kookaburra heralded the dawn, and celebrated a new day. When the kookaburra laughed during the day it announced that something or someone important was coming. The kookaburra is a good news messenger for all bush inhabitants.

Just as we have a tendency to read the voices of our landscape from a particular perspective—frequently anthropocentric—so, too, we read the voices in the various texts of the Bible that confront us from a specific perspective that reflects our particular context and worldviews. At unexpected moments within this inconvenient text called the Bible we are confronted by references to seas roaring, forests singing, skies celebrating and Earth rejoicing. Given our traditional view of such domains as voiceless objects, we have read these passages as metaphors—examples of poetic license. To resolve any momentary incomprehension, we routinely say that the poet gives domains of nature a voice to highlight the emotive dimensions of a given poem.

It seems to me, however, that these passages may also provide us with a clue as to how we might re-read the texts of Scripture from the perspective of these domains and, indeed, the viewpoint of Earth itself.

An alternative approach

In chapter 4 I outlined three basic dimensions of an emerging view of the natural world informed by ecology: *Earth is a precious living habitat, a fragile web of ecosystems, and a community of kin.* If we look more closely at the portrait of this worldview as Berry outlined it, we discern another dimension: Earth is a subject with a voice. Every being on Earth has its own voice and declares itself to the entire universe[1]. Earth is a planet full of voices: the diverse voices of all the beings making up the Earth community.

Those of us who have been educated in the Western world and absorbed its values will no doubt find difficulty with this perspective. We tend to accept dualism as reality; we see the world in terms of distinct oppositions: mind and matter, humanity and nature, heaven and Earth, animate and inanimate, spiritual and material, and so on. In this dualistic worldview, nature and the material do not have a 'voice' as we understand voice: nature is dumb and matter is mute!

Understandably, we have also read the Bible from the point of view of humans who see the beings and domains of the natural world as less than human, without the level of consciousness or communication inherent in, and characteristic of, humans. We have read the Bible listening for the voice of God, the voices of prophets or poets, and the voice of Christ. We have not read the text with a concern for the voices of Earth and the Earth community. We have been anthropocentric: we have read with a bias in favour of human interests and voices.

In the past 50 years, feminists have successfully challenged the way we read the Bible. They have made it very clear that throughout the history of Christianity, most interpreters of the Bible have been men and have read the Bible with a male bias. Male interpreters conveniently read texts as supporting the authority of men in religion and society. Women are expected to play a lesser role in society because 'the Bible tells us so!' Women in the Bible do not speak—they have nothing serious to say; their voices have been silenced by the way we have read and interpreted

---

1. Berry, *Great work*, 4.

the Hebrew, Aramaic and Greek texts, and how we have translated these texts into English.

Feminist interpreters also demonstrated that the biblical texts themselves were substantially the work of male authors with similar male biases. Understandably, therefore, male interpreters did not see ideas and views that did not fit with the way they saw the world and God. Feminist interpreters gave us reading strategies that have changed the way we read the Bible.

Among other things, they posed two crucial questions:

- Are there texts in the Bible where positive roles and voices of women are indeed present, but have been ignored or deliberately revised to fit a male perspective?
- How might we retrieve the voices of women who have been silenced, suppressed or suffocated by the original male authors, and readers of the texts?

Ecofeminists have taken a further step and recognised a social and symbolic connection between the oppression of women and the domination of nature[2]. Heather Eaton[3] contends that

> As European societies developed, the combined influences of the rise of science, the dualisms of the Christian worldview, the philosophy of modernity and the industrialisation of the economy became the cultural forces that entrenched the feminising of nature...The influence of hierarchical dualisms, a core piece of patriarchal ideology as described by Habel in this volume, is central to feminist critiques.

For Eaton and other ecofeminists, to read the Bible with Earth consciousness and woman consciousness means standing with the oppressed Earth.

Given the current worldview in which ecology now informs our values and orientation, I propose that we read the Bible posing two parallel sets of questions:

---

2. Rosemary Reuther, *God and Gaia: An Ecofeminist Theology of Earth Healing* (San Francisco: Harper, 1992).
3. Heather Eaton, 'Ecofeminist Contributions to an Ecojustice Hermeneutic', in Norman Habel & Shirley Wurst, eds, *Readings from the Perspective of Earth* (The Earth Bible 1; Sheffield: Sheffield Academic Press, 2000), 55.

1. **Are there texts in the Bible where the positive roles and voices of Earth and the Earth community are present, but have been ignored because of the anthropocentric mindset of interpreters?**

2. **How might we retrieve the voices of Earth and the Earth community silenced, suppressed or suffocated by human authors focusing first and foremost on human interests?**

Selected scholarly approaches

Some scholars defend the orientation of grey texts by re-reading them in the light of more favourable texts. The voice of God rather than the voice of Earth is their primary consideration; their assumption is that biblical writers will always portray God doing the right thing by humans and ultimately also therefore by creation. These scholars either rescue the import of grey texts by reference to texts they consider green or they justify the violence of God in nature as acceptable even if not palatable.

They argue, for example, that the mandate to dominate should be read in the light of the green text of Gen 2:15. They contend that the image of God that humans bear is intended to reflect peace and harmony toward nature. They soften the mandate to dominate in Genesis 1 by treating it as a version of the mission to serve in Genesis 2.

I would argue, however, that such conflicting texts should not be harmonised. We need to be faithful to the tradition of each text, no matter how one may contradict another. Grey texts are not green!

Other scholars develop a broad theology of creation that incorporates the various relevant texts to highlight God's creative presence, power and blessing, and to play down the import of those passages that portray God as destructive. God the compassionate Creator, they contend, may do whatever God wills with God's good creation.

This approach recognises that interpretation has been anthropocentric, focusing especially on the history of human salvation and ignoring the role of creation and the cosmos in the theological tradition. The agenda of this approach, however, is to uncover within the biblical and theological tradition, rich green texts that could bring ecology and theology into constructive dialog. As Santmire[4] asserts,

> I explore some of the biblical roots of the (classical Christian) story in an effort to rediscover the ecological and cosmic breadth and depth of the biblical witness over against the anthropocentric bias of much traditional biblical interpretation, an essential operation for any theological revisionist.

The interpretive framework proposed by Santmire, whose work I greatly admire, is what he calls a two-dimensional horizon: future and fullness, epitomised by an overarching theology of deliverance and a theology of blessing. He suggests that early texts dealing with a theology of deliverance lead to a land of fecundity, the promised land. Deliverance to this land is deliverance to a land of justice—a land that is first and foremost the Lord's land.

The problem with this broad scenario is that the blessing God first imparts to humans enables them to multiply so that they can dominate nature and subdue Earth (Gen 1:28). The blessing is fulfilled, it seems, when Joshua is said to 'subdue' the promised land by military conquest (Jos 18:1). The royal domination of that land by the Davidic monarchy is fraught with violence and dreams of the king 'ruling from sea to sea' and all other nations falling at his feet' (Ps 72:12–14).

> **For me these grey texts ask whether this kind of broad theological framework has taken adequate account of the injustice experienced by God's creation.**

Many scholars recognise the ancient cultural context and its limited cosmology when they examine the text. They read the relevant texts as products of a worldview which we no longer accept, and decide these texts can therefore be dismissed as obsolete and irrelevant. The only possible meaning of such texts, therefore, lies in a figurative reading, or a radical re-reading in the light of New Testament texts. These scholars dispense with the grey texts of the Bible as anachronistic, the remnants of an irrelevant 'primitive culture'.

---

4. Paul H Santmire, *Nature Reborn: the Ecological and Cosmic Promise of Christian Theology* (Minneapolis: AugsburgFortress, 2000), 10.

Another approach: Thomas Berry views the Genesis story in its cultural context as archaic and dysfunctional. He argues that we are between stories or worldviews. The emerging story is grounded, on the one hand, in the galactic mysteries of Earth's origins and a biocentric understanding of humanity's role in the universe[5]. In Berry's view, the new creation story totally replaces the Genesis story.

The serious alternative view proposed in this chapter differs from each of the above: it recognises that we are faced with an inconvenient book with grey texts that ought to be read honestly—as they are in the first three chapters of this volume. The approach to the text I am advocating recognises that today we read the text from within an emerging view of the world of nature informed by ecology and global warming. And it dares to pose the two basic questions enunciated above—questions relating to the explicit or suppressed voices of Earth and the participants in Earth community.

> **Rather than compromise or eliminate the grey texts in the Bible, our task is to re-read them from the perspective of Earth and to consider how we can use them to help us manage the current ecological crisis and the effects of global warming.**

Steps in green reading and analysis

At the outset, it needs to be emphasised that a green approach differs radically from typical approaches to texts about creation. The task before us is not an exploration of what a given text may say *about* creation, *about* nature, or *about* Earth. In a green reading, Earth is not a theme or topic for analysis. We are not focusing on ecology *and* creation, or ecology *and* theology[6]. An ecological reading demands a radical change of posture in relation to Earth as a subject rather than an object in the text.

The radical approach advanced here follows a basic process of interpretation involving suspicion, identification and retrieval.

---

5. Thomas Berry & Brian Swimme, *The Universe Story* (New York: HarperSan Francisco, 1992), 7.
6. Habel, 'Geophany'.

Suspicion

> First, we begin reading with the suspicion that past interpreters of the text—and potentially the writers of the text—focus on human interests rather than those of Earth or Earth community.

As Bible readers we have been conditioned to hear the voice of God or humans in the text rather than the voices of creation. Both biblical authors and interpreters are likely to have a dualistic orientation: they read the text in terms of humanity over against nature rather than humanity as part of nature. When we humans read the text, especially in the Western world, we tend to see ourselves as beings of a totally different order than all other creatures in nature. In other words, in our religious worldview God is on top, human beings on the next level and the rest, in hierarchical layers, at the bottom of the pyramid of living things.

We also tend to view nature as 'object'. For a long time, we have viewed nature and all its parts—both animate and inanimate—as the passive objects of many forms of human investigation, one of which is scientific analysis. This process has not only reinforced a sense of human superiority over nature, but has also contributed to a sense of distance, separation and otherness. The rest of nature—especially the so-called inanimate world—has been viewed as separate, other, and a force to be harnessed.

> In step one, we expose grey texts for what they are: texts that reflect an anthropocentric view of the natural world.

Employing this approach, then, we begin with the suspicion that we and past readers have studied the text with a bias that favours humanity and devalues the rest of creation. Given such a bias, we are unlikely to find many readings and interpretations that have dared to listen for voices from domains of nature other than those of humanity

Identification

> The second step in this process of interpretation is empathy or identification with Earth, the domains of creation, and members of the Earth community.

This is perhaps the step that requires the greatest leap of faith on the part of the reader; a step designed to overcome the bias of dualism that we find in ourselves, other readers and potentially within the text itself. As human beings we identify, often unconsciously, with the various human characters in the biblical story. Our identification may be empathetic or antipathetic: we can identify with the experiences of these characters, even if they are not necessarily individuals we admire or emulate.

The challenge we face is to identify with Earth, the domains of Earth or with members of the Earth community, and then to read the text from that perspective. Why? Because we now have a worldview that recognises we dwell on a living planet called Earth, that we are an integral part of the web of nature, and that we are kin with all creatures on this planet. We are born of Earth, made of Earth, and survive as living expressions of the ecosystem that has emerged on this planet. It is time we read as Earth beings in solidarity with Earth, not as God-like beings who happen to be sojourning on Earth.

When we identify with Earth and members of the Earth community, we are conscious of many injustices against Earth in numerous grey texts in the Bible—at the hands of both humans and God. It is natural that as readers using this approach we will ultimately take up the cause of the natural world. We will seek to expose the wrongs that Earth has suffered, largely in silence; we will discern, where possible, the way Earth has resisted these wrongs. When we identify with Earth we are more likely to hear the voices of Earth in the Bible, whether they are explicit, or suppressed by the bias of the dominant anthropocentric context.

> In step two we identify with Earth and dare to discern how Earth is treated by God or humans in grey or green texts.

I am acutely aware, however, that I remain a human being. I am not a tree, a mountain, a kangaroo or even a kookaburra. Any attempt to identify with Earth or members of the Earth community will remain less than ideal. That does not mean we should dismiss this step as futile. Far from it! We are part of Earth and can no longer ignore those nonhuman subjects, our kin in creation, who not only have intrinsic value; they have a voice in the text.

Retrieval

> **The third step in this approach is that of retrieval. As we read, identifying with Earth, domains of Earth or members of the Earth community, the text may first of all reveal a number of surprises about the non-human characters in the story.**

Earth or members of the Earth community may play a key role or be highly valued in the text, but because of the Western interpretative tradition we have inherited, that dimension of the text has been ignored or suppressed. Moreover, when we read about nonhuman figures communicating in some way—mourning, praising or singing—we have tended in the past to dismiss these expressions as poetic license or symbolic language, as metaphor. But these passages may well reflect how nature communicates in its own way

And when we identify with Earth and members of the Earth community, we recognise them as subjects with a voice. The task is to retrieve that voice. In some contexts their voice is evident but has been traditionally ignored by exegetes. In other contexts the voice of Earth is not explicit, but nevertheless present. These subjects play roles in the text that are more than mere scenery, metaphors or secondary images. Their voice—a voice that may not correspond to the language or words we commonly associate with the human voice—must be heard.

Discerning this voice may even take the form of reconstructing the narrative—as a dimension of the interpretation process—in order to hear Earth as the narrator of the story. In such a context Earth becomes an interpreter. This reconstruction is, of course, not the original text. I would argue, however, it is as valid as the numerous readings of scholars who, over the centuries, have reconstructed the literary sources, the historical events, or the cultural context of a text.

In a sense this process involves 'reading the silences' of the text. When we ignore these silences, by default we support the *status quo*, the mainstream anthropocentric thought of the author or reader. Like the silence of the abused child, the silence imposed on Earth or members of the Earth community protects the abuser; these silences can no longer be ignored. Retrieving the voice of Earth is a way to break the silence. A silence is not devoid of communication; day and night are silent in Psalm 19, yet their voices speak throughout Earth (Ps 19:2–4).

> In step three, having identified with Earth, we seek to retrieve
> the characters and voices of Earth and the Earth community in
> diverse texts—whether the texts are grey or green.

The essence of this approach is expressed quite clearly by Hilary Marlow
in an article on Amos[7]:

> The questions raised by the Earth Bible project include
> asking whether Earth is an active voice in the text or a
> passive lifeless entity, and if Earth is treated unjustly, and
> if so, to what extent that is acknowledged in the text. These
> concerns have promoted my re-examination of the text of
> Amos and a discovery that the natural world is an active
> participant in the Earth's story in this book.

Ecojustice principles

The analysis outlined above has evolved over a period of time. As many
readers may know, members of the Earth Bible team first formulated a
set of ecojustice principles in dialogue with ecologists. These principles
were articulated in *The Earth Bible* project and provided a basis for
ecological readings of key passages from the Bible. The five volumes of
The Earth Bible illustrate the initial stages in the development of a green
approach to reading the Bible. The six principles articulated in The Earth
Bible[8] are listed below.

---

7. Hilary Marlow, 'The Other Prophet! The Voice of Earth in the Book of Amos', in
   Norman Habel & Peter Trudinger (eds), *Exploring Ecological Hermeneutics* (SBL
   Symposium; Atlanta: SBL, 2008), 75.
8. Norman Habel, ed, *Reading the Bible from the Perspective of Earth* (The Earth
   Bible 1; Sheffield: Sheffield Academic Press, 2000), 24.

the principle of intrinsic worth: the universe, Earth and all its
   components have intrinsic worth/value

the principle of interconnectedness: Earth is a community of
   interconnected living things that are mutually dependent
   on each other for life and survival

the principle of voice: Earth is a subject capable of raising its voice in
   celebration and against injustice

the principle of purpose: the universe, the Earth and all its components
   are part of a dynamic cosmic design within which each piece
   has a place in the overall goal of that design

the principle of mutual custodianship: Earth is a balanced and
   diverse domain where responsible custodians can function
   as partners with, rather than rulers over, the Earth to sustain
   its balance and diversity

the principle of resistance: Earth and its components not only suffer
   from injustices at the hands of humans, but actively resist
   them in the struggle for justice

It is useful to indicate how these principles articulate with a green
analysis.

The first and fourth of these principles are especially relevant for an
appreciation of 'suspicion' as a basic consideration in our approach. It
has been traditional in most biblical interpretation that the nonhuman
creation has been treated as having less worth or value than humanity. A
mouse is not as valuable as a human! Neither is a walrus! Earth and its
components have not been viewed as having 'intrinsic' worth. At least,
that is the suspicion with which green readers now approach most past
interpretations and, potentially, the writers of this inconvenient text. For
most of human history, Earth has been regarded as created for the benefit
of humans rather than as part of wider cosmic design.

If, however, we dare to read any text recognising the intrinsic value
of Earth and all members of the Earth community within the cosmic
scheme of things, we are immediately faced with a range of alternative
values arising from within the text and from the perspectives of the
readers of the text. Suspecting the text and its interpreters have an
anthropocentric orientation is, therefore, not an arbitrary process: if we
affirm these principles, then we must name grey texts for what they are

and acknowledge that writers, readers and interpreters have devalued Earth and its component parts in the process.

The second principle connects with the process of identification or empathy. If we believe that there is an underlying interconnectedness between all ecosystems and living organisms, then we cannot avoid recognising our kinship with Earth and the Earth community.

The consequence of affirming this principle involves identifying, as we read the text, with Earth and the members of the Earth community. Then the question of whether these characters in the text are treated justly, or with genuine compassion, can no longer be avoided. Exploring this principle is no longer an intellectual exercise: the future of our participation/being in the Earth community is at stake. When we read with a mindset that seeks to empathise with the nonhuman characters in the text, and by looking at the text from their perspective, we discover what is happening to them.

The fifth principle is also relevant as we come to terms with our locus as Earth creatures in the interconnected ecosystems of Earth. Just as Earth nurtures all creatures on Earth through these ecosystems, all creatures nurture Earth and each other. Humans are an integral part of this mutual nurturing and care.

The third principle has probably evoked the most scholarly response. This principle recognises Earth as a subject with a voice that deserves to be heard as more than a metaphor. Our dualistic heritage has tended to reduce nonhuman domains to objects of analysis rather than subjects in their own right. Our anthropocentric values have tended to view texts that give Earth or the domains of Earth a voice as anthropomorphisms: they are merely a poetic way of giving parts of nature human capacities! These attributions are read as metaphors and are not to be taken literally.

The third principle is grounded in an ecological understanding of Earth as a living planet whose component parts communicate in a nonhuman mode; the research of Ursula Goodenough[9] demonstrates the remarkable range of forms of communication between all realms of nonhuman existence.

It is consistent with this principle, therefore, that we seek to identify not only passages that have a basic green orientation, but to retrieve the voices of Earth and members of the Earth community in grey and green

---

9. Goodenough, *Sacred Depths*.

texts. In many inconvenient texts their voices have been suppressed by writers and interpreters who use poetic excuses rather than recognise the ecological realities these texts describe.

The task of retrieval is also linked to the principle of resistance. Our goal is not merely to retrieve the voice of Earth celebrating or praising. Above all our goal is to recognise and retrieve the ways in which Earth has and continues to resist the injustices, imposed by God and humans, reflected in the text.

> These principles remain basic to a green approach, affirming our relationship to Earth and the Earth community. Our task is to apply the reading process outlined above in a way that is consistent with these principles and the emerging view of nature informed by ecology.

The basic challenge

How do we green biblical studies? Is a green reading of the Bible possible? Not if we continue to read grey texts and transform them in the light of green texts or convenient theologies. Not if we avoid appropriating the living realities of ecology that are beginning to inform our view of the natural world. Not if we cling to a faith that finds the spiritual primarily in another realm and not within our planet home.

To read from the perspective of Earth requires that we accept that our origins, identity and destiny are bound up with Earth. We are Earth beings, born of Earth, nurtured by Earth, and celebrated by Earth. We need to identify with Earth and the domains and creatures of Earth when we read grey texts that have been written to promote the interests of humans and their deity.

The steps proposed above are the beginning of a process facilitating our reading with a green orientation. And that means much more than asking what sort of cues the text provides to inform our care for creation, and more than only exploring texts that create a theology that affirms God as a Creator who sustains creation.

> A greening of biblical studies means standing in a very different place when we read: in reading green we stand with Earth and read for Earth and the Earth community. This stance is not a conversion: it is a return to the womb, to Earth as our mother, to the world we knew before we became alienated from nature.

To stand with Earth means to listen to Earth, to discern what is happening to Earth, and to take seriously what we hear or discover—even if that seems at odds with texts we have long taken as the final authority on matters of faith. To stand with Earth is to take up the cause of Earth.

You will have probably noted that in the opening three chapters I have already been applying step one of this process by exposing the grey anthropocentric dimensions of three groups of texts. In the final three chapters, I will apply the other two steps—although not in a rigid formal way. My goal is not only to retrieve alternative green texts—such as Gen 2:15—that have been largely ignored, but also to hear the voices of Earth, nature or the land suppressed by the grey orientation of the text or its interpreters.

> The confession of one writer[10] in our recent volume *Exploring Ecological Hermeneutics* is worth repeating: '*How can I have read the book of Amos so many times and not noticed the part the natural world plays within it? Why have I allowed my anthropocentric bias to muffle the voices of the rest of creation?*'

---

10. Marlow, 2008, 75

6

A Green Reading of the Mandate to Dominate

'It isn't easy being green'
Kermit the frog

A few years ago, there was a massive oil spill off the coast of South Africa. Gradually the oil moved towards Robin Island, near Capetown. Robin Island happened to be home for a large colony of fairy penguins. Moved by their consciences, a group of individuals rescued hundreds of penguins from the Island and relocated them about a thousand miles away on the Eastern side of the cape. They tagged three of the penguins to see what would happen.

After some weeks—when the island had been cleared of most of the oil spill—the fairy penguins began to return home. Not only did they swim the thousand miles home: they also took a detour South at one point to avoid swimming though a shark infested area. Their return says to us 'This is our place on the planet no matter where you try to relocate us. Respect us and our home.'

We are amazed at the feat of the penguins who had lived for so long on this island. Upon further reflection, however, we begin to recognise that a responsible group of humans demonstrated their green conscience.

One group of humans was willing to exploit Earth's oil resources and tolerate a spill that destroyed parts of nature; they were ready to subdue Earth at all costs. Another group was ready to act on behalf of nonhuman creatures rather than dominate them.

However, more of us need to be open to the voices of penguins.

The action of those who rescued the penguins represents a genuine Earth ministry, meeting the needs of their kin in creation. Quite a number of churches have initiated an Earth ministry in an effort to green the place where church members worship and celebrate. Some seminaries are exploring how they can green their ethics, their curriculum and their lifestyles.

The greening of biblical studies and Bible readings, however, remains problematic. Most writers and students of the Bible do not seriously read from the perspective of Earth or the perspectives of the diverse members of the Earth community. They do not identify with nature or domains of creation as they read. They do not hear the voices of nonhumans in the text. They do not employ principles basic to a green reading of the text.

In chapters 6–8, I will apply the steps of analysis outlined in chapter 5 to several of the grey texts discussed in chapters 2–4. This analysis does not claim to be as comprehensive as one might find in a Bible commentary or a detailed scholarly article; however, it is built on articles and studies that have applied this approach in greater depth.

The mandate to dominate

In the analysis in chapter 2, I demonstrated that Gen 1:26–28 is the work of a narrator who is concerned first and foremost with the interests of human beings. My analysis demonstrated that the orientation of the text is decidedly anthropocentric—as the first stage of a green analysis requires.

The author employs, moreover, the language of a dominating ancient Near Eastern monarch and depicts humans as royal representatives of God. The textual word from God to these humans is that they are to rule like kings and subdue nature—both the living creatures on Earth and Earth itself. They possess a divine mandate from God that justifies their separation from, and dominion over, both creatures and creation.

> **What happens if we identify with Earth and the living creatures of Earth rather than the humans in the text? What if we, as Earth beings, now dare to read from the perspective of Earth, our living abode and our biological place of origin? What if we empathise with Earth and Earth creatures rather than our fellow humans in the text?**

To demonstrate the force of this step, it is helpful to begin with the context of Genesis 1[1]. Our identification with Earth begins in verse 2. Earth is the first character introduced: 'And Earth was…'. Earth is depicted as an embryo, waiting in the dark primal waters; the wind of God's presence is hovering over the waters above. When we identify with Earth, we become one with Earth, waiting deep in the primal womb.

On days one and two, God creates light and sky: now there is light

---

1. See Habel, 'Geophany'.

for Earth to be seen and space beneath the sky for Earth to emerge. On the third day the waters part and Earth emerges from the waters below. Earth is revealed; Earth is born. In the words of the Genesis storyteller:

> And God said, 'Let the waters under the sky be gathered into one place and let the dry land appear'. And it was so. And God named the dry land Earth.
> (Gen 1:9–10)

Then God expresses delight by saying 'very good!'—or as Moses' mother implied when she used the same words: 'What a beautiful baby!' In other words, God affirms, values and celebrates the birth of Earth in these verses.

In the days that follow, God's delight continues as Earth becomes a partner in the creation process: the greening of the landscape and the filling of the Earth. Earth's ground is the source of all living things, all that is green and all air-breathing creatures: Earth's soil brings forth all kinds of vegetation; then animals emerge from the ground, fish emerge from the seas, and birds fill the air. Every living thing depends on Earth for life. All creatures have a common kinship that derives from Earth. Identifying with Earth in these verses leads to a sense of celebration with Earth as the mother who brings land, air and sea to life.

The grey text Gen 1:26–28 comes as a horrible intrusion in the plot of the narrative. Suddenly Earth is forced into the background. We seem to have a different narrator—one who has a totally different perspective on the world. His God ignores the former partner, Earth, and makes a new species called humans in God's royal image. This new creature has no connection or kinship with the Earth or the Earth creatures of the preceding narrative.

When we continue to identify with Earth as we read these verses, we realise that we are reading the words of a storyteller who has a totally different attitude to nature. This narrator wants to exalt humans—at the expense of Earth and the creatures of Earth. He portrays God as an overlord giving humans a mandate to dominate all life and to crush Earth under foot. Earth is depicted as a slave prostrate at the feet of human royals—an image made quite explicit in Psalm 8. Earth is no longer God's chosen partner; Earth has been traded in, as it were, for a new associate called humans.

> The narrator of Gen 1:26–28 has quite a different vision of God from that of the narrator of Gen 1:1–25. The God of these earlier verses celebrates the birth of Earth and works with her as a partner in the creation of life on Earth. The God of the mandate in Gen 1:26–28 forces Earth into the background and gives one species the right to crush Earth under foot.

What is the natural response of Earth to this anticipated treatment at the hands of humans? What is the suppressed cry of Earth in this text? We can legitimately expect to hear a cry for justice typical of those found elsewhere in the Bible. We can, I believe, hear Earth crying in the background:

> *Where is the justice in such a mandate? Why should I be subdued as if I were an enemy to be placed under foot? Why should the creatures I brought to life be treated as the slaves of human beings? Why? After all, I was a partner with God in creating all the living forms on Earth! I was happy to do God's bidding and give birth to other living creatures. Why should my children, who are all kin, be treated as beings of less value by humans? Where is the justice in this mandate to dominate?*

The mission to serve

When we move from Genesis 1 to Genesis 2, we are again confronted by a history of interpreters who ignore a central character in the story. They see the main characters as God, the man, the woman and perhaps the snake. They ignore the *adamah,* the ground. For clarity, in this green reading I will refer to the ground by its Hebrew name, Adamah.

The account begins by announcing that Adamah is not yet green because there was no one to 'serve' Adamah and nurture her—even though there was a spring rising from the midst of Adamah. In the beginning, there is a basic lack: the ground has no person or power to care for her. This situation moves God, the gardener, to take some of the soil from Adamah and, like a potter, mould the soil into a figure called an *adam,* a human being.

> In Genesis 2, humans were created from Earth for Earth. Earth was not created for humans!

God works with Adamah and greens the garden by causing a forest of beautiful and bountiful trees to grow, two of which were called the tree of life and the tree of knowledge. From that forest, rivers flowed in all directions.

The first scene of this story concludes when God gives the human the task of completing what was missing at the very beginning of the story. The human has the task of greening Adamah—or in the specific words of the text:

> Then the Lord God took the man and put him in the garden
> of Eden to **serve and preserve** it.
> (Gen 2:15 my translation)

In the next scene the animals and birds are also formed with the cooperation of Adamah. They are kin of the humans and their potential partners. The climax of the creation process is the making of the first woman who becomes the perfect partner for the first man. The humans are one with their animal and bird kin; they are united and equal in their role of serving Adamah. According to Daniel Hillel[2],

> This view of humanity's role accords with the modern
> ecological principle that the life of every species is rooted
> not in separateness from other forms of life in nature, but
> in integration with the entire living community.

The role of humans is to 'serve and preserve' Adamah. That is why they were created from Adamah. 'Serving' is what people did when they devoted their attention to a person or task: members of the court served the king; labourers served in the field; priests and worshippers served their God in the temple. Here humans are to 'serve' Earth—to dedicate themselves to Earth by attending to her needs.

But humans are also called to 'preserve' or 'guard' Earth, protecting her from oppressive or destructive forces, like those suggested by the mandate to dominate in Gen 1:26–28. There is an ancient Jewish tradition, grounded in this text, that emphasises the role of humans as guardians (*shomer*) of this planet, leasing it as valued property from God[3].

---

2. Hillel, *Natural History*, 243.
3. Daniel Swartz, 'Jews, Jewish Texts and Nature: a Brief History', in Roger Gottlieb,

> **In accord with the mission of Genesis 2.15, we would do well to declare ourselves guardians of the planet and take care of Earth as we would our mother.**

The subsequent scene in Genesis 3 is the famous dialogue between the smart talking-snake and the wise woman—a scene I do not plan to explore in this context. The outcome of this dialogue, however, shocks us when we identify with Adamah, not humans. Because of the actions of the humans, Adamah is cursed—to make humans suffer (Gen 3:17–18). We may hear the voice of Adamah protesting in the background:

> *Why should I be cursed: I am the ground from which animal life has been formed, from which green forests have emerged, and from which the first human was moulded. I am the lifegiver. Why should I be cursed? Am I like a mother who must suffer because of her children's actions?*

Before God sends the first humans out of the garden, however, God makes it clear once again that their mission is still to serve Adamah— even though it has been cursed. They are born of Adamah and will return to Adamah in death. Or in the words of Job,

> Naked I came from my mother's womb,
> And naked I shall return there.
> (Job 1:21)

If we dare to identify with Adamah—that domain of Earth from which all life is born, whether it be forests, frogs or humans—we hear the words of our mother, Earth, loud and clear.

> *Your mission from your maker is to serve and guard me, your mother. Your mission is to green the garden outside Eden. I have nurtured you; you have a duty to nurture me.*

---

ed, *This Sacred Earth. Religion, Nature and the Environment* (New York: Routledge, 1995), 98.

We can hear Earth's rewording of the mandate to dominate in Genesis 1:

> *And God said to me,*
> *'Let **us** make humans in our images:*
> *the image of Earth and the image of God;*
> *and let them recognise all living creatures*
> *as kin that emerged from me;*
> *and let them nurture me*
> *as I have nurtured them'.*

Efforts to green the mandate

A number of scholars try to make the mandate to dominate appear green. Their starting point is often the green commission to serve in Gen 2:15. In this text, God creates the first human being to 'serve and preserve' the garden. While the Hebrew term *abad* is sometimes translated 'till', its basic meaning is 'serve'. A comparison of the verbs in Gen 1:26–28 and Gen 2:15 is striking.

Gen 1:26–28	Gen 2:15
'rule' (*rada*)	'serve' (*abad*)
'subdue' (*kabash*)	'preserve' (*shamar*)

Here are two chapters, side by side; the verbs in these pivotal passages are diametric opposites: 'rule' is the opposite of 'serve' and 'subdue' is the opposite of 'preserve'. A number of scholars, however, cite the more convenient verbs in Genesis 2 ostensibly to shed light on Genesis 1. The verb 'rule' in Genesis 1 is therefore reinterpreted as 'rule with justice or compassion'; a common compromise translation is 'stewardship'. Humans are to be 'stewards' ruling Earth on behalf of God—the king in heaven.

Iain Provan's approach is typical—he discusses many of the same texts I have analysed above. He concludes:

> Genesis does not have in view absolute and unfettered power, which can be used as human beings will, with no moral restraint. Humankind's responsibility is rather to exercise 'dominion' on behalf of the God in whose world

they live—a just peaceable dominion, of the sort that is described for us in a psalm like Psalm 72[4].

A number of scholars, including Provan, have argued that since the text reflects royal language, the idea must be that humans will rule justly, since God the king is just. They cite Psalm 72 as an example of where the king is expected to reflect God's justice. A closer reading at this text, however, reveals an explicit reference to the king 'ruling' in verses 8–11: the psalmist prays that the dominion or 'rule' of the king will be from sea to sea and that, as a result, other kings will fall down at his feet and all nations will 'serve' him

In other words, the royal imagery and the language of 'rule' or 'conquer' in Genesis 1 or Psalm 72—even if camouflaged as 'stewardship'—portray an image of humans as the overpowering rulers of Earth, albeit on God's behalf. Stewardship, I would argue, still preserves a worldview that is in conflict with ecology. Stewardship is not necessarily green; nor does it respect Earth as a living companion. Or in the words of Clare Palmer, a leading critic of the stewardship model[5],

> Speaking of 'stewardship of the natural world' has important ecological consequences. Certain assumptions seem to lie behind or to be associated with it. Firstly, there is a strong sense of humanity's separation from the rest of the natural world. Following on from this there may be a cluster of beliefs: that the natural world is a human resource, that humans are really in control of nature, that nature is dependent on humanity for its management.

By explicating the image of God in the context of Genesis 2, some scholars argue that the harsh meaning of 'subdue' (tread upon), should be read in the wider context of the harmonious world of peace *(shalom)* that God is constructing. They even maintain that dominion—in the sense of the human capacity to multiply and fill the earthly habitat—is an ecological construct. The immediate context, which clearly indicates that 'filling'

---

4. Iain Provan, *Tenants in God's Land. Earth-keeping and People-keeping in the Old Testament* (Cambridge: Grove Books, 2008), 11.
5. Clare Palmer, 'Stewardship: a Case Study in Environmental Ethics', in Ian Ball et al, eds, *The Earth Beneath: a Critical Guide to Green Theology* (London: SPCK, 1992), 77.

the land enables humans to dominate nature and subdue Earth, seems to be conveniently ignored.

> I would argue, therefore, that these efforts to make the mandate to dominate green attempt a compromise between the basic meaning of both texts: the mandate to dominate and the mission to serve. Earth might well be heard complaining that humans acting as God's stewards may be thought to reflect a benign rule—but Earth remains the servant and humans are the bosses. But where are the compassionate children who are given the mission to serve and guard their mother?

The invitation to discern

The wise in the ancient Near East, the world of the Old Testament, have a genuine kinship with today's scientists. An integral part of their role: to observe phenomena both in society and nature in order to discern the essential features or driving characteristic of these phenomena. When they analysed a creature of the natural world, they called its basic characteristic or essence its 'way' (*derek*)[6].

In Job 39, God challenges Job to answer questions about the creatures of the wild to demonstrate whether he understands them and their 'ways'. God acknowledged that Job had a right to challenge the cruel sufferings that God had imposed on him, but surprisingly God responds by challenging Job's understanding of the mysteries in the natural world.

Especially relevant here is God's challenge relating to creatures such as wild oxen. Essentially God is saying that Job—like other humans, no matter how wise they are—does not have control or dominion over such animals. They are wild and free. Humans cannot domesticate or dominate them. This challenge is reflected in a delicious satire in which God asks Job to demonstrate that he can make a wild ox to 'serve' him, to babysit beside his crib, to do his farm work for him and finally to bring in the harvest.

> Is the wild ox willing to *serve* you?
> Will he spend the night beside your crib?

---

6. Norman Habel, 'The Implications of God Discovering Wisdom in Earth', in Ellen van Wolde, ed, *Job 28: Cognition in Context* (Leiden: Brill, 2003), 286–7.

Can you hold the wild ox in the furrow with ropes?
Will he harrow the valley behind you?
Can you rely on his great strength
And leave your toil to him?
Can you trust him to harvest your grain
And gather it in from the threshing floor?
(Job 39:9–12)

The significance of God's speech is that the Bible also includes texts that reflect ancient traditions that challenge the mandate to dominate in Genesis. Not only do we have a mission to serve in Genesis 2: the Bible also contains passages—such as Job 39—that include an invitation to understand the 'ways' or ecosystems of the natural world.

> **Job is forced to realise that, as a human being who claims to be wise, his mission is to discern—not to dominate; his mandate is to explore the mysteries of the natural world rather than exploit them. God calls Job to listen, respect and be humble before nature—not to be arrogant.**

And if we dare to identify with the creatures of the wild in this text, we hear them defying human efforts at dominion with wild laughter. The wild ass 'laughs at the furore of the city' and does not hear the shout of the taskmaster (Job 39:7). The ostrich likewise 'laughs at horse and rider' (Job 39:18); the charging horse 'laughs at dread' (Job 39:22). In Job 39 voices from the wild are retrieved; they challenge the very mandate that humans claim justifies human domination over them.

Clare Palmer writes[7]

> The animals are completely independent of humanity:
> the hawk, the mountain goats, the wild ox, the Leviathan;
> they are not made for humanity, not made to be humans'
> companions, nor even made with humans in mind. They
> live their own lives.

The way of Jesus of Nazareth

In many transformations the mandate to dominate has played a role in

---

7. Palmer, 'Stewardship', 70.

the exploitation and devaluation of our planet home. This grey text in Genesis 1 has a voice in the rhetoric and message of the church in its sanitised form called 'stewardship'. And the cry of Earth still rises: the mandate to dominate is not green but grey, not liberating but oppressive. A green reading of the mandate to dominate text reveals just how grey this text is, and allows Earth to give voice to the many injustices that this mandate has justified.

The mission to serve enunciated in Genesis 2 is being heard more widely and deserves our attention. In that mission the suppressed voice of Earth can be heard; in that mission the greening of Earth is again possible. In that mission we are called to be stand with Earth as kin, to hear her call, and to guard the planet we are commissioned to serve.

To harmonise the mandate to dominate and the mission to serve, I would contend, is environmentally foolish—and likely to produce a policy that is problematic to say the least: tolerating forms of domination under the guise of stewardship.

The divine portrait of the majesty and mysteries of the kingdom of the wild painted in Job 39 helps humans to recognise their place in this planet and to discern the wonders of its ecosystems. Sad to say, this text tends to be read by those interested in literature and philosophy rather than preachers and policy makers.

We are now faced with the question of how we should proceed, given that we have the decidedly grey texts such as Gen 1:26–28 and Psalm 8 in stark opposition to green texts such as Gen 2:15 and Job 39. Hearing and heeding the voice of Earth and her creatures crying out for justice in the face of God's mandate for humans to dominate and subdue may be enough, for many of us, to dismiss the mandate to dominate as environmentally irresponsible.

We may—once we have an inner awareness of our kinship with creation—naturally empathise with Earth in the green texts and choose to ignore the mandate to dominate.

The grey text in question (Gen 1:26–28), however, refuses to go away. For many, it has as much authority as the green texts; after all, it is the classic text in the Bible relating to the image of God (*imago dei*).

One resolution to our dilemma may be found, I contend, in the way of Jesus of Nazareth. Of course, Jesus was not aware of the ecological issues we face today—but the choice between dominating and serving was fundamental to his message. We remember his words to certain ambitious disciples,

> You know that among the Gentiles those whom they
> recognise as their rulers lord it over them and their great
> ones are tyrants over them. But it is not so among you; but
> whoever wishes to become great among you must be your
> servant, and whoever wishes to be first among you must
> be slave of all. For the Son of Man came not to be served,
> but to serve and to give his life a ransom for many.
> (Mark 10:42–45)

For Jesus the choice is clear: the new way that Jesus introduces into all relationships is that of 'serving'. The Gentile rulers he cites are typical: tyrants who dominate their people; they lord it over all their subjects. Jesus offers a diametrically opposite perspective on life: serving not ruling is the essence of his way. Being a 'slave' rather than a 'tyrant' is Jesus' mandate.

And this way is not merely one that Jesus enjoins on his disciples. This is the very way that he himself followed. He is the servant messiah. As a person appropriating the title 'Son of Man' as popularly understood, Jesus could have claimed great authority as the vision of the Son of Man in Daniel indicates (Dan 7:13–14). In Daniel, the Son of Man is 'given dominion' so that all nations may 'serve' him.

Jesus, however, claims to be a radically different Son of Man: a new Adam. He comes to 'serve' with his life and not to pursue dominion. His expression of serving has a deep connotation: Jesus is willing to go further than the faithful servant and give up his life for others. His serving means sacrificing his life. Jesus does not exemplify eternal dominion; Jesus' way of serving ultimately means giving his life as a 'ransom for many.'

> **The way of Jesus—serving rather than dominating—clearly
> stands in tension with the mandate to dominate in Genesis 1.
> I would go so far as to say that the way of Jesus supersedes the
> mandate to dominate.**

When we explore the opening chapters of Mark's Gospel, we discover a portrait of Jesus as the new Adam[8]. As the new Adam, Jesus is tempted by the devil/snake in the wilderness after which he lives with the

---

8. See J Marcus, *Mark 1–8: A New Translation with Introduction and Commentary* (Anchor Bible 27; New York: Doubleday, 2000), 168.

animals as Adam did in the forest of Eden. The new Adam refuses power over the dominions of Earth and resides with his kin in nature. Jesus is specifically said to be 'with' the wild animals (Mark 1:13), just as he is 'with' his disciples (Mark 3:14; 14:67). In chapter one Mark relates how Jesus heals Simon's mother-in-law; her immediate response is to 'serve them' (Mark 1:31).

If the way of Jesus is to serve rather than dominate—as articulated in Mark 10:45—the same principle applies in relation to all living creatures as well as to humans, to creation as well as to Christians. To follow the way of Christ, then, is to follow the mission of 'serving' Earth enunciated in Genesis 2, rather than dominating nature as expressed in Genesis 1. To follow the way of Christ is to choose the green rather than the grey texts as guides for life.

The challenge

The challenge before us is how to follow the way of Jesus of Nazareth and 'serve' and 'guard'—rather than 'dominate' and 'degrade'—our planet.

This challenge, I would argue, means having the courage to hear the cries of creation behind the grey texts of the Old Testament and to recognise them as valid voices. We need to listen to what they are telling us in the current climate crisis.

This challenge involves declaring that the grey texts of the Old Testament are superseded and are no longer valid as expressions of our faith in Christ.

This challenge requires us also to explore the relevant texts of the New Testament to ascertain whether they are grey or green, whether they reflect the way of Christ enunciated above.

The call to be guardians (*kaitiaki*) of the land is found among a number of Indigenous peoples. The Maori of New Zealand reenact the arrival of their ancestors from across the ocean more than a thousand years ago. They are confronted by four fierce guardian spirits: the guardians of the volcano, the ocean, the forest, and the wind. As they come onto the land they hear the cry of mother Earth: will you be guardians of my land? Their call echoes the cry of Earth in Genesis 2: will you be my guardians?

7

A Green Reading of the Mighty Acts of God

'I will never again curse the ground because of humans!'
Genesis 8:21

In December 2007, Kangaroo Island, south of Adelaide, was devastated by a mass of bushfires. On a hot dry summer day, an electrical storm enveloped the island, unleashing more than a hundred lightning strikes. These strikes lit fires throughout the natural reserves across the island. While this event was indeed a natural disaster, there is reliable evidence to suggest that the dryness of the island was intensified by global warming. Today, of course, no one on the island would read the disaster as a divine curse, a punishment for evil deeds committed by the island community.

Ironically, natural disasters of this kind are designated 'acts of God' in many of the legal systems of the Western world. When we consider similar events in many biblical texts, these 'acts of God' are not depicted as natural; they are acts of direct divine intervention for a specific punitive or salutary purpose.

A couple of months after the disaster, a visit to the vast areas blackened by the bushfires reveals that many of the trees and shrubs of the bush are sprouting again. Nature has begun to green the grey landscape. We may have had an immediate empathy for creatures like koalas and kangaroos who suffered in the initial blaze; with the greening of their habitat we anticipate their return with a sense of wonder.

What might a green reading of grey biblical texts about divine acts of destruction reveal? What green shoots might sprout from the grey textscape?

Cries of injustice in the flood

In my analysis of the flood narrative in chapter 2, I identified two introductions to the account: the first names the sin of human beings as the grounds for the flood; the second specifies that all flesh had 'corrupted its way'. Two corresponding decisions of God spell out the extent of the destruction to be effected by the flood—the first involving all humans and all animal life; the second involving all life on Earth and Earth itself.

Most interpreters of the flood narrative tend to ignore these destructive acts of God; they focus on the covenant promise with which the narrative concludes. Their focus is anthropocentric. They discern this promise as an indication that God has not only a personal covenant relationship with human beings on Earth; God also has a personal covenant relationship with other living creatures and with Earth—symbolising creation as a whole.

This covenant is understood to be an assurance of God's love for all creation. The covenant, according to Carol Robb for example, is extended to embrace all species. The natural world is thereby included in the history of salvation. This extended covenant is grounded in a theology that views people as 'a new humanity participating with God/ess as co-creators of the universe'[1].

A report of the World Council of Churches focuses on 'liberating life'. This report highlights the rescue of Noah and a few representative species from a watery death. The fact that all the rest of nature—animals, vegetation and Earth itself—were not liberated is ignored. The natural world does not seem to be included in the history of salvation, but rather subject to collateral damage time and again. As we demonstrated in Chapter 2, the liberation of God's people in the Old Testament is frequently not accompanied by the liberation of nature, a fact that few writers seem to consider.

Cries of the fauna and flora!

When we identify with the fauna and flora on Earth—or indeed with Earth itself—how does our understanding of the acts of God associated with the Flood change? What cries might we hear from the forests, fields and mountains of the land when the flood rises? Can we hear Earth mourning in this narrative as she does in other passages of the Scriptures?

From the perspective of nonhuman creatures, God's decision to obliterate them all is totally unjust. They have done absolutely nothing to deserve annihilation. They were declared 'good' along with the rest of creation in Genesis 1. The fact that representative species are finally

---

1. Carol Robb, 'Introduction', in Carol Robb & CJ Casebolt, eds, *Covenant for a New Creation: Ethics, Religion and Public Policy* (Maryknoll: Orbis, 1991), 18–21.

rescued in the ark hardly exonerates God for killing all nonhuman life on Earth because the human experiment was a failure. All fauna and flora are relegated to oblivion because God is ready to obliterate one species: human beings. The interests of humans seems to dominate the narrator's thinking.

The fact that God finally declares that humans will probably remain sinful, that the curse on creation ought to be removed, and that the seasons of the years will be sustained as part of the ecosystem of Earth, does not negate the need for God to say sorry for the injustices wrought on the fauna and flora of Earth. Their protesting voices can be heard as the flood waters rise.

> **Where is the justice in drowning infant animals—whatever the species—just because humans have done evil things? Where is the justice in depriving innocent baby birds of habitats so that they drown and die? Where is the justice in submerging the vibrant vegetation of the land until it chokes and disappears? Why make the land grey because human beings have black hearts?**

And we can hear the groaning of the *adamah*, the ground:

> *So God has said sorry. God has promised to never again curse me because of the sins of humans. I accept God's apology. I welcome his promise to sustain the ecosystems and the seasons. I only pray that this God will actually keep this promise to never again curse the ground—or life from the ground—because of humans.*

Yet there is a green dimension—however brief—to the closure of the first grey flood narrative: the God who said he was in pain before the flood because of human sin (Gen 6:6) now seems to express a similar remorse after the flood. We seem to meet a God who empathises—or even suffers.

> When the Lord smelled the pleasing odour, the Lord said in his heart, I will never again curse the ground because of humankind.
> (Gen 8:21)

The significant aspect of this text is not only that God admits that in the past the divine approach was to curse parts of creation because of what humans had done; God changes this approach. Creation should not suffer for human sin. Even more significant, perhaps, is that God here refers to the cursing of *adamah*—the ground cursed because of Adam. In other words, the divine policy of injuring Earth because of humans—operative since Eden—has now been reversed. The question to be explored later: is this reversal of the way God acts evident in the rest of the Old Testament—and in the New Testament?

It is interesting to note that just as we hear the silent voice of Earth in the text, the narrator hears the silent voice of God—'in the heart' of God, not shouted across the receding waters of the flood.

Cries of Earth

In the second version of the flood account, the narrator indicates that God discerns chaos and corruption in the living creatures of Earth; it extends beyond human beings. One resolution of this chaotic state of affairs would be to modify the nature of each living creature—including humans—so that they would all be true to God's original design. Every living being would then live according to the 'way' God implanted within each of them.

Instead, God decides to destroy all life and start again. Only one human—Noah—is found to be true enough to his way to survive; his family survives with him.

While the destruction of all life seems to be totally unfair, the 'corruption' of Earth by means of a flood seems to be absolutely unjustified.

Earth is not the sinner.

Earth is not the criminal!

Earth is not the corrupt partner.

Why then is Earth 'corrupted' by God? Why should Earth suffer the consequences of the chaos and corruption of living creatures?

Admittedly, after the Flood, God seems to say sorry. God makes a promise with all humans, with all fauna and flora on Earth, and with Earth itself: 'I will never again send such a flood'. This divine apology, however, does not remove the memory of the injustices wrought against

Earth. The mourning cries of Earth are latent in the text. If we empathise with Earth we hear her groaning.

> *Where is the justice in God 'corrupting' me because humans are corrupt? Where is the justice in violating me: I was God's partner in bringing the fauna and flora into being? Where is the justice in drowning me in the waters of death when alternative means of restoring life are at God's disposal? I hear God saying sorry. I pray that God will keep this promise and never corrupt me—or any of my domains—because of human wrongdoing.*

These cries for justice from Earth and all the domains of Earth deserve to be heard! Earth has been the victim of 'acts of God'—acts that are intolerable. And just as with the precious divine promise, God reverses the policy of destroying Earth because of human wrongdoing.

Yet God goes beyond saying sorry; beyond reversing past policy; beyond promising not to cause a comparable flood in the future. God makes a covenant.

And this covenant suggests that there is a green dimension at the end of the flood story after all.

A covenant is an agreement between two or more participating parties. Most biblical covenants are between God and humans; this covenant involves more than humans.

In the past this covenant has been read as a promise **to** living creatures and Earth, and as a promise **to** humans that God will not destroy all living things in a global flood.

The text, however, declares that the covenant is **with** Noah's descendants, **with** all living creatures and **with** Earth.

> God said, 'This is the sign of the covenant I will make **between me and every living creature** that is with you, for all future generations: I have set my bow in the clouds, and it shall be a sign of the covenant **between me and the Earth'.**
> (Gen 9:12–13)

The wording makes it clear that all living creatures and Earth are not passive objects of God's promise; they are recognised as active subjects in a covenant relationship with God. This covenant recognises creatures and creation as more than background scenery in the plan of God.

Finally, God relates directly to creatures and creation as covenant partners.

Whether or not there are grey texts that portray a rather different picture of God's relationship to creation in the rest of the Old Testament, this one text reveals an underlying kinship between Creator and creation that is potentially green.

If God can make Earth a genuine partner in a covenant, we humans can do the same. If we were to engage in a covenant dialogue with Earth, what would our mutual covenant embrace?

Cries of the waters in Egypt

As we indicated in chapter 2, the Exodus includes an extended series of events including: the plagues; the departure from Egypt; the crossing of the Reed Sea. Most interpreters are anthropocentric and focus on the plight of the oppressed humans, the Israelites. Yet the injustices suffered by the many domains of nature at the hand of God cry out for recognition. The groaning of creation persists under ten plagues, ten curses.

Turning the water to blood until there is blood throughout the land, the Nile waters cry out: *we are innocent!*

Covering the land as a plague, frogs—a symbol of what is green—cry out: *we are innocent!*

Swarming unnaturally throughout the land, gnats, flies and locusts cry out: *we are innocent!*

Suffering deadly pestilence and festering boils, livestock cry out: *we are innocent!*

> *We hear the land, the waters, the living creatures and the skies groaning in unison. We feel used and abused by God. We suffer and cause suffering through no fault of our own. Where is the justice or compassion in that?*

If we ask whether God has a personal connection with the realms of nature, we are led to the famous hymn that celebrates the mighty acts of God in delivering Israel from Egypt (Exodus 15). This portrait, however, depicts God as a mighty warrior not as compassionate creator. Instead of God's breath being the gift of life, it is a weapon of destruction. The blast of God's nostrils causes the waters of the sea to pile up and stand in a heap. Another blast from these nostrils sends the waters back to cover the Egyptians. The right hand of God opens Earth to swallow the enemy. Nature is manipulated by God in order to rescue the people of God.

Is this Earth's response?

> *I am happy that you employed my winds to disrupt the flow of the waters and destroy people? I am happy that you opened my deeps so that I could swallow humans. I am happy...Or am I?*

The 'great work' God performed in the liberation of Israel from Egypt is depicted as monumental. As a result the people feared YHWH and believed (Exod 14:31).

There is, however, no liberation or affirmation of Earth and the domains of Earth in the Exodus narrative. They are simply used by God to punish Egypt and to liberate Israel. Their innocent cries are suppressed green voices in a decidedly anthropocentric and ethnocentric narrative.

Cries of Earth in the prophets

The prophets have long been hailed as the champions of justice, denouncing the wrongs committed against the widow, the poor and sojourner. Are there any indications that injustice against Earth and the creatures of Earth is also recognised by the prophets? Are there any suggestions that the prophets recognise YHWH's covenant with Earth and her animals, announced in Genesis 9?

In a few places, the prophets seem to be sensitive to the cries of creation; they hear Earth mourning. Jeremiah, who wonders how long the land will mourn, hears YHWH's cry:

> They have made it (the land) a desolation;
> Desolate it mourns to me.
> The whole land is made desolate,
> And no one lays it to heart.
> (Jer 12:11)

When locust plagues invade, Joel hears the ground mourning, the animals groaning, and the wild animals crying out to God (Joel 1:10, 18, 20). These expressions of anguish, however, are relatively rare. The dominant image is of YHWH sending a range of natural disasters to

punish, or to provoke repentance. Amos reminds Israel that though
YHWH sent droughts, blight, mildew, locusts and pestilence, Israel
refused to repent (Amos 4:6–10).

One prophet whose oracles seem to have a green consciousness is
Hosea. His classic word from God is announced in chapter 4:

> Hear the word of the Lord, O people of Israel;
> for the Lord has a case against the inhabitants of the land
> (*erets*).
> There is no faithfulness and loyalty,
> and no knowledge of God in the land (*erets*).
> Swearing, lying and murder,
> and stealing and adultery break out;
> bloodshed follows bloodshed.
> Therefore the land (*erets*) mourns,
> and all who live in it languish;
> together with the wild animals
> and the birds of the air,
> even the fish of the sea are perishing.
> (Hosea 4:1–3)

When we read this passage from the perspective of the land or Earth
(*erets*) as a key character in the text, we become aware that, in the court
case God is holding against the people of the land, the experience of
the land becomes a testimony to the injustice perpetrated by the people.
Earth, the skies and other domains of creation are often witnesses to the
covenant in the ancient Near East.

In Micah, the mountains, the hills and the foundations of Earth are
summoned to plead their cause in YHWH's case against Israel (Micah
6:1–2). They are genuine participants in the covenant with Israel, not
simply token symbols, part of the scenery. In Hosea, the mourning of
the land is public testimony to Israel's violation of the covenant with
YHWH; in Hosea, the land is a living witness to the covenant.

Some scholars argue that Earth is not only the witness against Israel in
the covenant trial that God is holding, but also the agent of punishment.
Melissa Tubbs Loya writes:

> When Hosea 4:1–3 is read from the perspective
> of the land, the Earth emerges as an active agent,

simultaneously imposing and suffering the sentence of YHWH's *rib* (court case) against Israel. In this prophetic oracle, creation is not simply scenery in which the story of Israel's relationship is played out. Rather, creation actively mourns the subversion of the created order[2].

> **The cries of Earth in the prophets are green; they reflect isolated moments when the suppressed voice of creation breaks into the consciousness of the prophets. These are not reconstructions of an empathetic interpreter: Earth mourns, the prophets hear...and we ought to listen.**

The cries of Earth in these green prophetic texts are significant for several reasons. First, they cause us to recall the original curse pronounced on Earth in Eden (Gen 3:17). From the time of the narrator remembering Adam's situation to an era of prophets sensitive to the suffering of creation, we recognise Earth suffering because of humanity and with humanity. Mother Earth continues to suffer and cry out on behalf of her children.

A second reason why these texts are relevant is the testimony to their voice. While some may object to the process of retrieval where we articulate the voice of Earth or members of the Earth community in a given context, the prophets provide a bold precedent when they hear and acknowledge the cries of creation, especially the mourning of Earth. The cries of Earth in these texts are more than metaphors; they are invitations to hear the cries of creation wherever nature has been abused, whether in the biblical tradition or the contemporary environmental crisis.

The green God of Psalm 104

Can we retrieve any green texts where God bonds with nature rather than destroys it outside the prophets? Psalm 104, I suggest, reveals a radically different presence to the God of destructive mighty acts outlined above. Instead of God 'outside creation' who intervenes with acts of devastation, we discover God 'in creation': God permeates the ecosystems of the atmosphere, the rivers, the seas, the mountains and

---

2. Melissa Tubbs Loya, '"Therefore the Earth Mourns": The Grievance of the Land in Hosea 4.1-3', in Norman Habel & Peter Trudinger, eds, *Exploring Ecological Hermeneutics* (SBL Symposium, Atlanta: SBL, 2008), 62.

the plains. The psalmist has such a sense of God's presence deep in creation that he dares to take a hymn to the ancient sun god of Egypt and modify it to express the brilliance of YHWH as the very light and life, the being 'in, with and under' the universe.

In Psalm 104 we discover God/our God enveloped in light appearing in the sky, God's tabernacle in space. We find God riding high in the wild winds and on the swirling clouds. We find God in the mountains, God stirring the streams to gush forth water for the animals, God providing vegetation as nesting places for birds. We see God in the sky sending showers down on the mountains and across the land. We watch God in the land, grassing the fields to provide food for cattle and humans. And there's more: bread and oil and wine to make life enjoyable!

The list of God's creative impulses occurring daily in creation goes on and on! It includes God helping young lions find prey and inducing the darkness so that wild animals of the forests can creep about safely. God is even found deep in the ocean, sporting with a great sea monster to celebrate life. The cry goes up: 'There go the ships and Leviathan you formed to sport with'. And it is precisely this celebrating of God in the midst of creation that the psalmist desires: 'May YHWH rejoice in his works!' (Ps 104:31).

Perhaps the most significant revelation is God's breath as the atmosphere. God breathes and there is life; God withdraws breath and creatures return to dust. The spirit or breath of God is the atmosphere that 'renews the face of the *adamah* (ground)' (Ps 104:30). Here there is no cursing of *adamah*—as in Genesis 3; or of the land—as in the Old Testament histories of God's mighty acts. In Psalm 104, God is the vibrant blessing that permeates all of creation.

As the psalmist says,

> When you hide your face they are dismayed;
> when you take away your breath, they die
> and return to the dust.
> When you send forth your breath they are created;
> and you renew the face of the ground.
> (Ps 104:29–30)

A fresh reading of Psalm 104 retrieves an exciting green text that proclaims a radically different God from the one who liberated Israel from Egypt—and left a trail of destruction in creation.

We might even say that to be green in Psalm 104 is the work of the spirit; to be green is to be spirit-filled or spiritual!

And returning to the dust is returning home as Adam and Eve discovered (Gen 3:19). There is no duality here; the breath of God is the very wind, air and atmosphere that bring our planet to life.

> **The breath of God—the atmosphere of Earth—is the life-giving spirit permeating all creation. And that breath brings the** *adamah*—**the fertile ground—to life, greens the landscape and infuses it with God's presence.**

Psalm 29 was also probably adapted from outside sources: a very ancient hymn probably addressed to the Canaanite storm god Baal. Another psalmist recognised God's presence in nature, and transformed the original nature song into a hymn to YHWH. In this psalm, the voice of YHWH is the thunder that rumbles across the storm waters with frightening power. The God who is thundering is the God whose presence is revealed in the glory: a storm cloud filled with fire. The thundering voice of YHWH is so powerful it shatters the tall cedar trees and strips forests of their foliage.

With the thunder comes the lightning: another dimension of God's powerful presence. The lightning flashes; the lightning strikes and forests burst into flames. And in the sanctuary above, celestial beings respond with a chorus of 'gloria': in the thunderstorm they celebrate the brilliant fiery presence of God in nature!

The psalmist acclaims YHWH as the king of the storm, enthroned above the storms waters. This is not a portrait of the God who manipulates the storm, the waters and the wind to deliver Israel from Egypt; this God revels in being deep in the ecosystems of nature.

And the final hope is not mighty acts of victory over Israel's foes but the blessing and peace that come in the aftermath of the storm. That 'peace' is *shalom*, a term that might well be interpreted as ecosystems balanced with blessings!

The acts of God in Jesus' acts of healing

The numerous passages in the Old Testament that report the acts of God destroying parts of nature as God's people are rescued or punished, make the Old Testament an inconvenient text indeed. For many scholars in the past, these acts of God—especially those associated with the

Exodus—have been viewed as the focal point of the Old Testament. The creation stories are considered secondary or introductory. The great contribution of the Old Testament was its focus on the acts of God in history as distinct from the presence of God in nature—an image of God typical of other gods in Israel's immediate cultural environment[3].

Is there, within the New Testament, a change of orientation towards the acts of God more in line with the orientation of Psalm 104? Is the spiritual presence of God's breath renewing creation also found in the New Testament? Do the acts of God represented in the work of Jesus Christ reflect a kinship with creation or are they a demonstration of power over nature that may include destructive dimensions?

The healing miracles of Jesus are positive deeds that demonstrate Jesus' intimate interaction with the human body; often a spiritual dimension is implicit in the acts of healing. When Jesus heals the paralytic, for example, his capacity to forgive sins is also demonstrated (Luke 5:17–26). In his report to John the Baptist, Jesus informs John that, with his miracles, he brings 'the good news to the poor' (Luke 7:22). When a woman is healed after touching Jesus' garment, the emphasis is not on Jesus' miraculous power: her faith that has made her well (Luke 8:48).

Nevertheless, one healing story, however, seems decidedly grey: a man possessed by violent demons could not be contained and was frequently driven into the wilderness. When Jesus confronts them, the demons beg him not to send them back into the abyss where they would disappear and perhaps be destroyed. They beg Jesus to let them possess a herd of swine feeding nearby. Jesus agrees and the possessed swine plunge down an embankment and drown. Jesus tells the man to return home and inform his community 'how much God has done for you' (Luke 8:26–39).

This healing is interpreted by Jesus as an act of God: God is at work in Jesus' acts of healing. The destruction of the swine, however, seems to be unwarranted collateral damage. Why should the innocent swine suffer? Why should they be possessed? Why should they drown? They were innocent animals who just happened to be in the neighbourhood! And while some may feel less than comfortable identifying with swine, they are as much our kin in creation as any cute kitten.

When Jesus' stills the storm we meet him interacting with nature in a special way. The boat is about to sink as the waters from the storm fill

---

3. See, eg, Claus Westermann, *The Genesis Accounts of Creation* (Philadelphia: Fortress 1964).

the boat. Meanwhile Jesus, sleeping somewhere in the rocking boat, is oblivious to the crisis. When the disciples wake him, and he rebukes the wind and the waters, there is an immediate calm. He chides the disciples for their lack of faith. They, in turn, are amazed at the power of Jesus' word (Luke 8:22–25). Jesus can command winds and water. Jesus' action creates calm, however, rather than a raging wind that forces back the waters as God did at the Reed Sea. Unlike the image of God moving deep within the forces of nature, as projected in Psalm 104, Jesus controls the wind and the water with his word; there is no indication in this narrative that he is present in the forces of creation.

The act of God becoming flesh

When we turn to John's Gospel, however, we encounter a radical understanding of who Jesus really is. We meet someone who is more than a bold prophet with powerful words who can still storms or expel demons. In Jesus, we meet God as incarnate word. Is the image of God in John 1 grey or green? Are Earth and creation valued or devalued in this classic text?

As distinct from the Genesis 1 account of creation, John moves the primordial back prior to the existence of the physical components of Earth, water and wind that are already present in the opening verses of Genesis (Gen 1:2). In an earlier article I wrote[4]:

> In John 1 the creation of everything (*ta panta*) in the physical world is covered in summary fashion in one verse (John 1:3). The text does not focus on the seven-day creation scenario in Genesis 1. The bold story of Earth in Genesis 1 is ignored; the 'good creation' that God discovered is not even mentioned. The emphasis in John 1 seems to be on what the Word brings to creation rather than on creation itself.

The difference in orientation between Genesis 1 and John 1 seems be that the former is physical and the latter spiritual. In Genesis 1 life and light refer to the domains of the physical universe; in John 1 'life' is explicitly

---

4. 'Ecojustice Challenge: 'Is Earth Valued in John 1', in Norman Habel & Vicky Balabanski, eds, *The Earth Story in the New Testament* (The Earth Bible 5; Sheffield: Sheffield Academic Press, 2002), 78.

identified as 'the light of humans': a dimension of the universe that enables them never to walk in spiritual darkness. The light of the Word conquers this darkness and continues to shine in the world. In Genesis 1 the darkness is not evil; to render it so is to devalue it.

John 1:1–13 seems to present a cosmology that devalues Earth and the physical cosmos. The superior realm is heaven—the spiritual domain 'above' from which the Word apparently comes to create, to bring life, and to redeem. The cosmos—and especially Earth—is viewed as an inferior domain 'below', clouded in spiritual darkness and in need of redemption.

Is that redemption only for humans?

The crucial passage that demands our attention is John 1:14.

> And the Word became flesh and lived among us, and we have seen his glory, the glory as of a father's only son, full of grace and truth.

Is this text green? Is 'flesh' in this text but a temporary abode of the Word that passes from 'above' to 'below'—and always back to 'above' again?

Or does the transcendent, the Word from above, enter the material world of flesh, become an integral part of it and thereby revalue it? Does my suspicion about the dualistic orientation of this text reflect my male Western heritage?

Elaine Wainwright suggests that we read John 1 in the light of a different primordial story of the beginning: Proverbs 8[5]. In Proverbs 8 Wisdom or Sophia is present to celebrate the creation of all the physical domains of Earth. Sophia also celebrates with the Creator, rejoicing in the inhabited universe[6]. Wainwright, reading with empathy for Earth, wonders whether the first century readers heard echoes of Proverbs 8 and other Wisdom texts just as readily as memories from Genesis 1. They may have heard the opening of John 1 as follows:

---

5. Elaine Wainwright, 'Which Intertext? A Response to an Ecojustice Challenge: Is Earth Valued in John 1?', in Norman Habel & Vicky Balabanski, eds, *The Earth Story in the New Testament* (The Earth Bible 5; Sheffield: Sheffield Academic Press, 2002), 76–82.
6. Wainwright, 'Which Intertext?', 84.

> In the beginning was Sophia and Sophia was with God. She
> was in the beginning with God and all things were made
> through her, and without her was not anything made that
> was made.

The Earth-affirming background for John 1 that Wainwright evokes
suggests that we can retrieve an alternative understanding of 'flesh'
and the 'world' (*cosmos*) as not necessarily negative counterparts to the
'spirit' and the 'spiritual realm' above[7].

If, on the other hand, we recognise that *logos*, the Greek term for Word,
was clearly masculine in Greek thought, we are faced with another
dilemma: the *logos*—the mind or divine impulse in the cosmos—stands
in opposition to the body or flesh of the cosmos. In New Testament Greek,
the *logos* was viewed as masculine, superior and divine—the Word who
is God. The flesh was considered feminine, inferior and transitory[8].

What happens when the Word 'becomes' flesh? In the wider context
of our readings, flesh may refer to all that lives. 'All flesh' is destroyed
in the flood. It is this very 'earthy stuff' of this material world that the
Word 'became' in the incarnation.

Elsewhere in John's Gospel, Jesus seems to reflect the popular view
that flesh is inferior when he says: 'That which is born of the flesh is
flesh!" (John 3:6); 'It is the spirit that gives life, the flesh is useless' (John
6:63). In John 1, however, we hear that God is born of flesh! More than
that, God becomes flesh! Flesh is redeemed!

By this act of God, we have a radically new revelation of God's
relationship with creation. Edwards writes[9]:

> Flesh evokes the whole world of interrelated organisms.
> It suggests that in becoming flesh, God has embraced all
> creatures in the interconnected web of life. A New Zealand

---

7. See, eg, Vicky Balabanski 'John 1—The Earth Bible Challenge: an Intra-Textual
   Approach To Reading John 1', in Norman Habel & Vicky Balabanski, eds, *The
   Earth Story in the New Testament* (The Earth Bible 5; Sheffield: Sheffield Academic
   Press, 2002), 89–94.

8. Alan Cadwallader, And the Earth Shook'—Mortality and Ecological Diversity:
   Interpreting Jesus' Death in Matthew's Gospel', in Denis Edwards & Mark Worthing,
   eds, *Biodiversity and ecology: an interdisciplinary challenge* (Adelaide: ATF Press,
   2004), 4–18.

9. Edwards, *Heart of Faith*, 58.

theologian comments on this line of thought: 'To say that God became an Earth creature, that God became a sentient being, that God became a living being (in common with all other living beings), that God became a complex unit of minerals and fluids, that God became an item in the carbon and nitrogen cycles' (Darragh, 124).

> **In short, when the Word became flesh, God became a piece of Earth—like Adam!**

In addition, the apparent opposition between the eternal masculine *logos* and the transitory feminine flesh, between the superior divine mind and the inferior earthy matter, is overcome. God unites with and permeates the very stuff of nature. The incarnation is that radical moment when we learn that the God—who has long been portrayed as intervening from a position outside of creation—is in fact operating inside creation: Jesus Christ is an explicit revelation of that reality.

God joins the web of creation—and relates to nature in a radically new way. In some of the green texts in the psalms, God is envisaged as permeating the domains of creation. In the text of John 1, God 'becomes' one specific piece of Earth: a human called Jesus, whose body is composed of the very same elements and organisms that are part of any living flesh. In this act of God we gain a clear revelation of God identifying with and permeating creation, rather than disturbing or destroying it.

The revelation of God 'in the flesh', then, enables us to discern the same green dimension to God in green creation texts—though not in the grey texts that portray a deity acting with violence towards nature. The incarnation of God in Jesus is anticipated in those creation texts where God's breath and being have been present—incarnate—from the beginning. This God has, and continues to become, incarnate throughout history. McFague writes[10],

> The world is flesh of God's 'flesh'; the God who took our flesh in one person, Jesus of Nazareth, has always done so. God is incarnate, not secondarily but primarily. Therefore, an appropriate Christian model for understanding creation is the world as God's body. This is not a description of creation

---

10. Sallie McFague, *A New Climate for Theology. God, the World and Global Warming* (Minneapolis: Fortress, 2008), 73.

(there are no descriptions); neither is it necessarily the only model. It is, however, one model that is commensurate with the central Christian affirmation that God is with us in the flesh in Jesus Christ, and it is a model that is particularly appropriate for interpreting the Christian doctrine of creation in our time of climate change.

The challenge

The challenge before us is how the green text of John 1:14 may assist us in interpreting the texts, so common in the Old Testament, that depict the destructive acts of God. Instead of engaging in conflicts that involve violent acts of liberation and judgement, the act of God assuming human flesh and surrendering to violence, including death, reveals God's compassionate presence in creation. When the Word becomes flesh, God joins the web of suffering creation and suffers with creation. Acts of divine violence against nature may be viewed as heroics of the past. We may even say that in Jesus Christ, God disarmed God's self and disowned the way of violence towards nature reflected in the Old Testament. Dorothea Soelle writes[11]:

> In Jesus Christ, God disarmed himself. God surrendered himself without protection and without arms to those who keep crying for more and more protection and arms. In Jesus Christ, God renounced violence. In Christ, God disarmed unilaterally. God took the first step.

The challenge before us is to recognise that the God who became flesh and suffered in that flesh did so for all creation. In the light of John 1:14 may we declare obsolete those grey texts where God acts mightily to liberate or punish, and in doing so destroys domains of creation?

---

11. Dorothea Soelle, *Thinking about God: an Introduction to Theology* (London: SCM, 1981), 96–97.

In recent years, a number of churches throughout the world have begun celebrating a new season of the church year: *The Season of Creation*. A central focus of this season is celebrating *with* creation rather than simply give thanks *for* creation. Another focus is the eternal presence of Christ in creation. An affirmation of our Christian faith in this season: 'We believe God became a piece of Earth, like Adam, and lived among us as Jesus Christ' (see www.seasonofcreation.com).

8

A Green Reading of Promised Land Texts

'There is a piece of land in me,
And it keeps drawing me back like a magnet to the land from which I
came. Because the land, too, is spiritual. The land owns me.'
George Rosendale

The land owns me! This declaration of George Rosendale is typical of the
orientation of Indigenous elders in countries like Australia[1]. This deep
and abiding kinship between the elders and the land that owns them,
stands in stark contrast to the perspective of invading peoples who lay
claim to the land as property and expect ownership. Many Indigenous
peoples believe they belong to the land; the land does not belong to
them. When they walk the land, they read the landscape and the land
responds. They listen to the land. Is there any of this sense of kinship
with the land in the Bible?

In our Western world, land is a complex concept. It can refer to that
domain of Earth made green with vegetation and other forms of life; it
can be understood as property belonging to a given party; it can be the
very source of living organisms—both in the Bible and biology; or it
can be territory claimed and cleared by its owners. Rarely do Western
peoples believe the land owns them or that the land is spiritual in any
way.

Land, as distinct from Earth, is subject to claims of ownership. The
land is mine! Such a claim can be made by individuals, tribes or nations.
In Lev 25:23 even God makes such a claim to land. And in the context of
the 'promised land syndrome', the claim to ownership is grounded in a
divine charter based on a patriarchal promise.

The specific claim that God has 'given' the land to Israel may also
reflect ancient legal authority. According to Orlinsky[2], the Hebrew term
natan, to 'give', can refer to the allocation of land as a legal grant of

---

1. Rainbow Spirit Elders, *Rainbow Spirit Theology*, 12.
2. Harry Orlinsky, 'The Biblical Concept of the Land of Israel: Cornerstone of the
   Covenant between God and Israel', in LA Hoffman, ed, *The Land of Israel: Jewish
   Perspectives* (Notre Dame: University of Notre Dame Press, 1986), 27–64.

property (Orlinksy 1986). The promised land is ostensibly a land the ancient Israelites claim to own both by divine right and legal sanction.

Listening to the land

In chapter 3 we recognised that the promised land ideology played a role in the colonial invasion and exploitation of Indigenous lands. The book of Joshua represents a divine precedent justifying these land grabs.

Is there anything green about Joshua? What do we discover when we read this book from the perspective of the land and empathise with the land itself?

If, like the Indigenous elders, we read the landscape and listen to the cries of the land, our understanding would be quite different. We might hear the land crying.

> *Why does this invading deity need to engage in holy war? Why devote cities and landscapes to destruction rather than preservation? Why, after rescuing his people from Egypt with mighty acts of destruction, does this God feel constrained to do the same to the peoples and the land of Canaan?*

If we focus on the culmination of the narrator's account of the heroics of Joshua (Joshua 24), we may possibly discern an appreciation for the land as gift and blessing. But given the earlier orientation of the book we suspect that this closing text will also be anthropocentric, reflecting the promised land syndrome of the rest of the book.

Joshua's final deed is to establish a covenant between his household and YHWH, a very jealous God who will tolerate no other gods. All the households of the Israelites have been assigned their specific plots of land. The time has come for the people to say thank you to God for giving them a land with vineyards and olive orchards that the Israelites did not plant and for the cities they did not build. They have been given a productive land—even if, ironically, they have destroyed much of it. In the face of various options, Joshua declares that his personal household will make a covenant with the warrior God, YHWH, and declare this deity their one and only God.

When the covenant agreement has been written in the book of the law of God, Joshua reads the text. A large stone—part of the new land—is erected to be a witness to the covenant agreement.

There is, however, no covenant with the land as such. The land becomes the property of the various households of Israel. Yet, the very fact that the large stone witnesses the covenant indicates that Joshua is not only aware of the covenant treaty ritual, but that a rock representing the land actually 'hears' the words of the covenant with YHWH. The stone is not merely a ritual object but represents the voice of the land.

> Joshua said to all the people, 'See this stone shall be a witness against us; for it has heard all the words that the Lord has spoken to us; therefore it shall be a witness against you, if you deal falsely with your God'.
> (Josh 24:27)

As noted earlier, Abraham had made a covenant with Abimelech to keep covenant faith with the land as well as the people of the land. The land itself was part of the deal, part of the covenant. Abraham made a covenant with Abimelech and the land. Abimilech is quite explicit that

> as I have dealt loyally with you, you will deal loyally with me *and the land* where you have resided as an alien.
> (Gen 21:23)

Joshua appears to ignore that covenant between Abraham and Abimilech. Joshua and his household are ready to 'serve' YHWH; but there is no agreement to 'serve' the land, which was the mission of Genesis 2. Apart from the rock included in his covenant with the people, Joshua is a grey text to the very end.

Surely we can hear the land crying out in protest.

> *Before you Israelites invaded with your warrior God, I was sustained by the Canaanites. They and their gods had a kinship with me, with the land—a mutual fostering of fertility and blessing: They nurtured me and I nurtured them. They and their gods had rites for renewal of the fauna and flora. They and their gods were in tune with the life of the landscape.*
>
> *Why should my people be damned for worshipping gods that they believe made the promised land a blessing for the invaders? Where is the justice in that?*

*Then you invaded me and claimed that your God had given
you a land belonging to others. You engaged in a holy war of
destruction, crushing the people and the produce of the land. You
'subdued' the land under the mandate to dominate granted you
by your God (Josh 18:1). You treated the creatures of the land
as the spoils of war, not the blessings of the Creator. Where, O
Joshua, is the justice or compassion in that?*

There is little that is green about Joshua. Even though the promised land
is a dominant theme, the land as such is denied a genuine voice and
remains merely the property of the invaders. When we identify with
the land we feel humiliated and sad. When we empathise with the land
we hear her cries of injustice, cries that many Indigenous peoples have
heard for centuries.

> **There is no promise to the land in the Book of Joshua—there is
> only a promise that the invaders will own the land.**

The land is mine

The so-called Sabbath text of Leviticus 25–27 is often cited as a green text
with a radically different orientation to that of the promised land texts
in Joshua and Deuteronomy. In the Leviticus text, life in the promised
land is to reflect a genuine care for the land as an agricultural domain.
After six years of productivity, the seventh is to be a Sabbath year in
which no farming is to occur. As a result the land has a chance to rest
and regenerate.

After seven sequences of seven years, the fiftieth year is declared a
year of jubilee in which liberty is proclaimed to all inhabitants in debt or
slavery. The fiftieth year also becomes a year of rest. This jubilee year is
declared holy, an extra year of rest.

Blessings from the land are dependent, however, on the people keeping
the statutes of God's covenant. When Israelites get into financial trouble
they may choose to sell their land. In the year of jubilee, however, they
or their relatives can redeem it. Ultimately, the land may not be sold in
perpetuity to another household; God says: 'the land is mine; with me
you are but aliens and tenants' (Lev 25:23).

It is significant that God, in this text, is the landowner—a role that seems
to echo the world of Eden. On the Sabbath year, the land returns to its
owner: the divine landlord. The tenants have no rights or responsibilities

during that year. By returning the land to its divine owner, the Israelites acknowledge their absolute dependency on the goodness and authority of their landowner. Do these peasant farmers and their God, who rest along with the land, identify with the land in the Sabbath year? Is the land a living reality with rights to be respected?

Another significant feature of this text is the symbolism of the land as sanctuary. In Exod 15:17, the land of Canaan is designated YHWH's entitlement and sanctuary (*miqdash*), even before any shrine or temple is built in the land. In Lev 16:2, the Israelites are enjoined to keep my sabbaths and reverence my sanctuary.

> **In this Leviticus context, the sanctuary is the land of Canaan where YHWH, the landowner resides. The land is YHWH's 'dwelling place'. In this abode, YHWH 'walks' among the inhabitants.**

This 'walking' of God in the land recalls the 'walking' of God in the garden of the first humans (Gen 3:8): the same unusual Hebrew expression is used in both texts. Like Eden, the land is God's sanctuary. Here YHWH is no absentee landlord who resides in heaven, but a deity who dwells in the land, walks through it and celebrates its Sabbaths[3].

> I will grant peace (*shalom*) in the land...and I will make
> my dwelling place in your midst and I will not abhor you.
> I will walk among you, and be your God and you shall be
> my people.
> (Lev 26:6, 11–12)

Clearly this Leviticus text stands in sharp contrast with the promised land texts of Joshua and Deuteronomy. The divine landowner has a concern for his land, which is also his sanctuary. His sanctuary is in the care of peasant farmers who must keep covenant with their landlord if they are to flourish and survive. Keeping covenant, especially the Sabbath laws, means keeping the land green.

There is, however, a significant difference between the Leviticus text and the mission of Genesis 2. In Leviticus the people serve their divine landlord while in Genesis 2 humans are to 'serve' the land itself. Listening to the land we might well recognise a sense of relief on the part

---

3. Habel, *Land Ideologies*, chapter 6.

of the land: in Genesis 2 there is a covenant commitment to the promised land rather than a promise of conquest and ultimate ownership. In the Leveticus text YHWH owns the land. This is the perspective of the peasants who work the land and not those in power—whether they be kings, warriors or city dwellers. This text presents an agricultural ideal. The question remains: was this ideal ever realised in practice?

Returning to the land of promise

The promised land tradition also persists in the writings of prophets who anticipate the return of God's people from exile in Babylon. Some prophets, like Jeremiah, seem to envisage a restoration of the land rather than a radical transformation (Jer 33:10–11). Are these prophetic dreams of a new promised land really green?

In the visions of Isaiah 40–55, we sense that the agonies of the past, represented by the wilderness, will be overcome by God with radical acts of transformation. The summons to prepare a way in the wilderness (Isa 40:3) is answered by sympathetic responses from God and the wilderness itself. When the poor need water, God promises to open rivers in the bare heights, turn the wilderness into a pool of water, fill the dry land with springs and plant several varieties of trees in the desert (Isa 41:17–19). What is naturally a dry landscape is transformed miraculously into a fertile forest.

Especially powerful is the promise of God to perform a miraculous intervention comparable to the way created through the Reed Sea when the Israelites escaped from Egypt (Isa 43:16–21). This proposed way in the wilderness is so new it will put past miracles in the shade! The waters created in the wilderness and the rivers in the desert will evoke praise—not only from God's people, but also from the wild animals, the jackals and ostriches. The wilderness, which is the epitome of desolation and aridity for God's people, becomes a domain transformed into fertility and celebration. Memories of past trials in the wilderness after the exodus from Egypt will be forgotten.

> **There is a sense in this Isaiah passage that the grey dimensions of the Exodus narrative are reversed. YHWH's destructive acts of intervention are no longer part of the plan.**

Those deeds of liberation and destruction associated with the Israel's exodus from Egypt are to be forgotten in the light of YHWH's new plan of salvation. This plan is so radical that the creatures of the wild will celebrate rather than call for justice. Instead of a way through the waters of the sea that brings destruction, YHWH will make a way through the desert to bring life.

> I am about to do a new thing;
> now it springs forth, do you not perceive it?
> I will make a way in the wilderness
> and rivers in the desert.
> The wild animals will honour me,
> the jackals and the ostriches;
> for I give water in the wilderness,
> rivers in the desert
> to give drink to my people,
> the people that I have formed for myself
> so that they might declare my praise.
> (Isa 43:19–21)

The way in the wilderness is more than a route to salvation; it is a virtual return to Eden. The waters that were agents of pollution and destruction in the exodus event now become participants in the revival of both the Israelites and the creatures in the wilderness

This salvation will survive even when heaven vanishes like smoke and Earth wears out like a garment (Isa 51:6). Significantly, it is the God who claims to have created the skies above and to have spread the Earth below—where life is animated by divine breath—who claims now to be performing this new thing in history and in nature. The seas and the desert are invited to respond in song (Isa 42:5–13). In this context, God transforms nature to facilitate the salvation of God's people by walking them through the desert: a salvation that supersedes the miraculous crossing of the Reed Sea (Isa 43:1–3). The mighty acts of God transform the natural ecosystems of the desert into ideal lush domains comparable to Eden.

How does the land itself respond? Perhaps her appreciation of being transformed is less than rapturous:

> *Walk through my wildernesses and listen to the songs of the wild,*
> *observe the ways of creatures who survive by their wiles in the*
> *wild, and celebrate the mysteries of lands where humans do not*

*dominate. Why demonise my wilderness and then seek visions
that transform her into a different ecosystem? My wilderness —
whether it happens to be a desert or a forest — is to be preserved as
part of God's sanctuary. Yet God bringing water to my wilderness
is preferable, I suppose, to having my water turned into blood!*

The future of the promised land

Throughout the prophets there are numerous portraits of how God will
transform the promised land at some point in the future. A common and
troublesome theme of these portraits is that the natural is transformed
into the unnatural[4]. Instead of a restored ecosystem we see a distorted
ecosystem. Instead of investing nature with its original value, God
manipulates nature for alternative ends. The new heaven and the new
Earth of Isa 65:17–25 anticipate that Jerusalem will not only be full of
joy, but also be inhabited by people who live for hundreds of years.
The land will enjoy the so-called peaceable kingdom where the natural
relationships between wolves and lambs, and between oxen and lions,
will no longer exist:

> The wolf and the lamb shall feed together,
> the lion shall eat straw like the ox;
> but the serpent—its food shall be dust!
> They shall not hurt or destroy
> on all my holy mountain' says the Lord
> (Isa 65:25)

The prophet dreams of a green world which recalls the ecosystem of
Eden, a world where there was no conflict between creatures. The
prophet clearly has Eden in mind, but some dimensions of reality will
never change, it seems: snakes will still eat dust!

In Ezekiel's vision of the restoration of the land, the image is again
one of an idealised landscape like Eden where the land is tilled, sown
and inhabited. Passers by will exclaim

---

4. Sibley Towner, 'The Future of Nature', in *Interpretation* 50 (1996), 27–35.

> This land that was desolate has become like the garden
> of Eden; and the waste and desolate and ruined towns
> are now inhabited and fortified'.
> (Ezek 36:35)

This idealised scene of Israel's peaceful habitation, however, is balanced by a ghoulish feast following the conquest of Gog. Ezekiel is expected to summon all the wild animals for a sacrificial feast on the mountains of Israel. The wild animals are invited to 'eat the flesh of the mighty and drink the blood of the princes of the Earth' (Ezek 39:18). The feast will continue until all the wild animals are drunk with the blood of the enemy. Here the wild animals are not creatures who enjoy life in their natural environment—they become vehicles of divine vengeance and jealousy for the holy name.

In the famous vision of the new temple of Jerusalem, including details of its design and ritual (Ezek 40–48), there is a specific scene depicting the transformation of nature (Ezek 47). Unlike a typical shrine, water flows out from below the threshold of the temple toward the East (Ezek 47:1). In spite of the beauty of the symbolism in this scene, it depicts a world that does not correspond to the normal river ecosystems of Earth. The waters are manipulated to create an unnatural centre for the land.

The miraculous character of this river is its capacity to transform a sea of stagnant waters into fresh water, and to create a healthy habitat for fish and other water-living creatures. The banks of the river produce all kinds of food-bearing trees. The miraculous character of the trees is demonstrated by the fact that their leaves do not wither and their fruit never fails. Amazingly, they do not follow the eco-cycle of known fruit trees; they bear fresh fruit every month because 'water from the river flows from the sanctuary' (Ezek 47:12). Once again, we have a vision of a future where God transforms the natural ecosystems of Earth to create a unique other-than-natural domain in the midst of the land.

Surely we can hear the land protesting again.

> *Where is the fruitful and natural land promised to the patriarchs?*
> *Why does God, whom I thought walked through my fields*
> *and valleys as my protector, need to create a sanctuary that is*
> *different—separated—from to the rest of nature? Why does God*
> *suggest a future where the new promised land is itself alien to*
> *the very creation God has celebrated in the past? These images*

of a transformed land, Earth, or even heaven may be grand and glorious but they are hardly green — at least not as I have known green in the past.

In these dreams of the future the original green creation that God declared 'very good' is abandoned by the Creator and replaced by an unnatural new creation. Why?

Resistance texts in the New Testament

The grey and green texts cited from the Old Testament in relation to the promised land pose a major challenge as we engage with the New Testament writers. Do they view the promised land as property to be appropriated, owned and exploited? Is there any sense of kinship with the land or Earth? Is the promised land to be restored and made 'green'? Or is something else foreshadowed? Is there any criteria linked to Gospel texts that assist us in choosing between grey texts that view Earth as property to be owned and exploited, and green texts that affirm Earth as a sanctuary or as a compassionate partner in the struggle against domination and destruction?

It is plausible that in his manifesto in Luke 4, Jesus declares that the spirit is moving him not only to proclaim social justice for the poor and oppressed, but that ecojustice is also on his agenda: his mission is also to 'announce the year of the Lord's favour' (Luke 4:19). Many scholars are agreed that Jesus refers back to the year of jubilee in Lev 25:10, a green event, a text declaring the land as God's sanctuary and a domain where God walks through the land.

For Jesus to announce the year of jubilee as part of his mission is to celebrate not only the freedom from debt associated with that year but also a sense of belonging to the land as God's abode and source of blessing. Even if Israel sins, God will 'remember' both the covenant and the land as God once promised to remember the covenant with Earth (Lev 26:42). Jesus' quotation of Isaiah 61 in his manifesto in Luke 4 omits the reference to the Lord's 'day of vengeance'; the year of the Lord's favour means peace and blessing for people and land; there is no need for violent punishment.

The biggest challenge facing New Testament readers, it seems to me, are those texts which seem to indicate that the Earth is disposable and therefore of relatively little value.

In these contexts, the promised land is no longer Canaan or planet Earth as we know it; it is some other distant domain. This Earth may even be dissolved (2 Pet 3:10) and a new heaven and Earth will appear, a universe, for example, without any sea and without any sun or moon to shine on a new Jerusalem (Revelation 21).

A number of scholars, however, have discerned that the book of Revelation is a visionary work written in the face of Roman domination that included blatant environmental evils. Barbara Rossing, for example, reads Revelation 12 as an example of Earth resisting the ecological domination of Rome. At first it appears that the following verse from Revelation 12 is a grey text.

> Rejoice then, you heavens,
> and those who dwell in them!
> But alas for the Earth and the sea,
> for the devil has come down to you with great wrath,
> because he knows that his time is short.
> (Rev 12:12)

The context makes it clear, however, that the 'alas' experienced by Earth is a typical lament like those proclaimed by the prophets. Earth is in sympathy with a suffering creation and willing to resist the evils imposed by dominating humans—and their gods. In this vision, Earth finally comes to the aid of the woman giving birth; Earth boldly swallows the river pouring from the dragon's mouth (Rev 12:16). As Rossing has discovered, texts in Revelation may in fact be green:

> Revelation's primary polemic is against Rome. Even while Rome claims to reign over the entire Earth, as illustrated by its own imperial propaganda, Rev 12:16 furnishes a glimpse of an Earth that is not a compliant subject of imperial domination. Earth's heroic swallowing of the dragon's river in Rev 12:16 is an action that model's the sixth Earth Bible principle, the principle of resistance[5].

---

5. Barbara Rossing, 'Alas for Earth! Lament and Resistance in Revelation 12', in Norman Habel & Vicky Balabanski (eds), *The Earth Story in the New Testament* (The Earth Bible 5; Sheffield: Sheffield Academic Press, 2002), 181.

Barbara Rossing also demonstrates that there is a radical difference in the orientation between two texts: 2 Peter and Revelation. In terms of the preceding discussion, the relevant texts of 2 Peter are grey and those of Revelation are green. In the words of Rossing[6],

> To summarize: Within the spectrum of early Christian apocalyptic literature, Revelation and 2 Peter represent two very different eschatological perspectives on the 'end'. Whereas 2 Peter envisions an end to the earth and whole created world, Revelation envisions an imminent end to the Roman imperial world.

The writer of the book of Hebrews, however, seems to reinterpret Abraham's hope of a promised land in an even more radical way. He maintains that ultimately Abraham, like all of us, looked for a 'better country, that is, a heavenly one' (Heb 11:16). The promised land is apparently relocated in heaven, and life on Earth becomes a pilgrimage. We even sing words that echo this reading:

> Guide me O thou great Jehovah,
> Pilgrim through this barren land.

These visions of the new heavens and Earth—a heavenly homeland— seem to anticipate that God will transform or recreate nature in such a way as to eliminate many of the domains and ecosystems that are vital to life as we know it. If we identify with the land in this context, we wonder why the land—once God's sanctuary, where God walked and blessed its gardens—should be replaced. If we empathise with Earth we find such visions demeaning and hear Earth responding:

> *If you read the landscape you will discover I are not 'barren' land*
> *but an exciting ecosystem to be embraced and celebrated.*

The groaning of creation

The challenge remains. Joshua depicts a promised land that is a conquered land, property to be owned and exploited; Leviticus describes the land

---

6. Barbara Rossing, 'Hastening the Day when the Earth Will Burn? Global Warming, Revelation and 2 Peter 3', in *Currents in Theology and Mission* 35, 2008, 308.

as God's sanctuary, where God the landowner prescribes laws that will keep the land green; several prophets depict a future for the land that represents an unnatural radical transformation of the natural order. How do we decide which texts to select as viable memories or visions to endorse and advocate in the current ecological crisis?

Perhaps the most relevant green text in this context is the message of Paul in Romans 8. This chapter has long been recognised as potentially green. The opening section, as translated by Byrne[7], reads:

> I consider that the sufferings of the present time are a small price to pay for the glory that is going to be revealed to us. For **creation waits with eager longing** for the revealing of the sons (and daughters) of God. For **creation was subjected to futility**—not of its own volition but on account of the subduer—in the hope that the creation itself would be **set free from its slavery** to decay in order to share the freedom associated with the glory of the children of God.
>
> For we know that the entire **creation has been groaning together in the pangs of childbirth** right up until now; and not only creation, but we ourselves, who have the first fruits of the Spirit, **groan inwardly** while we wait for adoption, the redemption of our bodies.
> (Rom 8:18–23)

Byrne demonstrates that Paul's allusion to creation in this passage has been problematic for many interpreters; it does not seem to sit easily in a book that focuses so strongly on the fate of humans[8]. Byrne[9] argues that Paul's teaching is based on the

> principle that, because human beings were created along with the non-human created world and given responsibility for that world, they share a common fate with that world. When the situation of human beings deteriorates, so does

---

7. Brendan Byrne, 'Creation Groaning: an Earth Bible Reading of Romans 8.18–22', in Norman Habel (ed), *Readings from the Perspective of Earth* (Earth Bible 1; Sheffield: Academic Press, 2000), 197.

8. Byrne, 'Creation Groaning',194.

9. Byrne, 'Creation Groaning', 197.

that of the rest of creation, and, vice versa, when it goes
well, the creation shares in the blessing.

The interdependence of humans and creation is indeed apparent in this
text. I would argue, however, that creation rather than humans is the key
character in Paul's analysis of the world scene.

First, it is creation who is waiting with eager longing for the good times
that will follow the current suffering of humans. There is, in creation, an
empathy of hope as well as an empathy of suffering. Creation is depicted
as a character with the same genuine emotions as humans: they face the
future together.

Second, it is creation who has been subjected to futility. As scholars
agree, this is probably an allusion, first of all, back to the curse imposed
by God on creation because of the sin of Adam (Gen 3:17–19). Creation
itself was an innocent participant; it knew the futility of being subdued
by God's curse. The reference to 'subduing', however, suggests that the
real culprit is humanity. The mandate to dominate and 'subdue' creation
given to humans in Gen 1:26–28 is exposed by Paul as contributing to
the suffering of creation.

Third, creation will also participate in the liberation that has been
associated with humans. The interdependence of humanity and creation
is intrinsic to Paul's understanding of the future, even if he does identify
them as separate subjects.

Fourth, creation is portrayed in feminine terms as a mother groaning in
the pangs of childbirth. All the curses, wounds and injustices experienced
by creation are interpreted as more than sufferings per se: they are signs
of a deeper movement taking place in the ecosystems at risk. Creation is
also in travail. There is a future beyond the current apparent futility—a
reality to which the barren Sarah testifies (Rom 4:19).

Fifth, the groaning of creation is not experienced alone. If we are
sensitive to our identity as 'first fruits of the spirit', as living proof
of a rebirth in creation, we will be groaning along with creation. In
addition, the Spirit is groaning with prayers of intercession, 'with sighs
too deep for words' (Rom 8:26). God, as the Spirit deep in creation, is
participating in the pain, and anticipating the new creation emerging
from this creation.

> Rom 8:18–27 is a powerful green text. Here Paul hears creation
> taking a lead in the struggle against grey forces and traditions!
> And this text, I suggest, leads the way for us to read all visions
> about the future of creation.

This Romans 8 text is particularly significant in a green reading context: instead of a sweeping divine intervention that eliminates Earth or transforms the natural into the unnatural, creation itself, together with a groaning humanity and a suffering Spirit, are anticipating a healing of the wrongs done to creation. The present creation is an integral part of the process for birthing a green future. Creation continues!

The groaning at Calvary and beyond

Most of the events surrounding the death of Jesus at Calvary involve human activities. There are a number incidents, however, that suggest creation too was involved. The Gospels record that at about noon, when Jesus was on the cross, darkness came over the whole land for about three hours (Mark 15:33; Luke 23:44).

This event is an expression of the sympathy of creation reflecting the prophetic memory of Earth's mourning outlined in the previous chapter. Jeremiah announces, for example, that when creation has all but returned to chaos, Earth mourns and the heavens grow black (Jer 4:28). The heavens turning black reflects the response of creation to the situation: darkness above corresponds to the mourning of Earth below; the darkness over 'the whole land' is an expression of creation groaning with the suffering one on the cross.

Susan Miller[10] contends that the 'voice of Earth is heard through the descent of darkness and the Earth identifies with Jesus' suffering'; she argues this moment anticipates the return of the Son of Man in the future. This darkness reflects the empathy of Earth: Earth's sufferings are part of the birth-pangs of creation and anticipate a new day for creation.

Alan Cadwallader[11] demonstrates that Matthew's portraits of the curtain of the temple being torn from top to bottom, Earth shaking and

---

10. Susan Miller, 'The Descent of Darkness over the Land. Listening to the Voice of Earth in Mark 14:3–9', in Norman Habel & Peter Trudinger, eds, *Exploring Ecological Hermeneutics* (SBL Symposium; Atlanta: SBL, 2008), 128.
11. Cadwallader, 'Earth Shook', 53.

rocks splitting open reflects the empathy of all three tiers of the ancient cosmos at the moment of Jesus' death. As he writes,

> Rather than viewing the events surrounding Jesus' death as an eschatological promise or initiation for the benefit of human beings alone, these events become the total cosmic setting that determines the significance and understanding of Jesus' death. Mortality is rendered not a human preoccupation but a cosmological event that, significantly, has earth at its centre. Only in connection with the heavens, the earth and the deep does, indeed can, death have any meaning. The anthropocentric preoccupation with escaping death by withdrawal from the cosmos to another place is denied by Matthew.

One tradition in Christian theology emphasises the suffering of Christ on Calvary and views the resurrection and ascension of Christ as evidence that Christ has moved beyond this Earth to reign above in glory, in the promised land of heaven. After all, the Christ who humbled himself and became obedient unto death on the cross has been exalted and given a name above all other names (Phil 2:4–11). His suffering for and with creation seems now to be over!

The green texts identified above have tended to locate God in, with and under creation; Creation is God's sanctuary, world—or even body. The grey texts locate God outside of creation, intervening and interrupting the natural ecosystems of Earth. Romans 8 highlights a groaning that is common to creation, humans and the Spirit in creation: here we have an alternative to the popular notion that God, in Christ, now rules above and is no longer suffering deep in creation below.

There is, moreover, another text that summons our attention: Col 1:15–20. In this passage it is clear that Christ—the true image of God—was prior to all creation, and is the creator of the universe. But more than that, all things (*ta panta*)—the entire cosmos—are held together in him. Jesus' presence permeates the universe; his energy unites the cosmos. The resurrected Christ, liberated from the body of Jesus of Nazareth, is present in all bodies. And ultimately, says the text,

> Through him (Christ) God was pleased to reconcile to himself all things, whether on Earth or in heaven, by

making peace through the blood of his cross.
(Col 2:20)

The Christ who suffered on the cross is here revealed to be the Christ
in creation whose suffering effects the reconciliation and healing of all
creation—not just humans. And if, as this text announces, the suffering
Christ permeates the wounded creation, the process of reconciliation
and healing continues. This green text reveals God at one with creation,
ready to identify with a groaning creation rather than exercise dominion
or destruction. Balabanski[12] writes,

> The cosmic Christ who spilt his blood on the cross, and
> was emptied of power, is the icon of God in the sense that
> he did not prioritise his life and power over others. In
> doing so, Christ demonstrated that there is…the possibility
> of respecting the impulse to life in the other in continuity
> with one's own impulse to life, and also choosing to forego
> power for the sake of the kinship of the *pneuma* (spirit) we
> share.

> **The suffering Christ who fills the cosmos is a deep healing
> impulse with whom we need to connect. We may do so as we
> listen to the groaning of creation and the cries of the spirit in our
> ever warming atmosphere.**

The challenge

The green texts of Romans 8 and Colossian 1 could be explored further;
these passages offer guidelines for reflecting on other texts. The basic
criterion for a green reading—in line with the central message of this
text—is whether endorsing the perspective or principles in a text will
intensify the groaning of creation or contribute to its liberation and
ultimately ours as well. We need to ask, as we consider any text, whether
it is in continuity with the tradition of 'subduing' creation or whether it
supports the hope that there will be a rebirth of creation when we groan
together with creation and the Spirit.

---

12. Vicky Balabanski 'Critiquing Anthoprocentric Cosmology: Retrieving Stoic
"Permeation Cosmology" in Colossians 1.15–20', in Norman Habel & Peter
Trudinger, eds, *Exploring Ecological Hermeneutics* (Atlanta: SBL, 2008), 159.

Which of the promised land traditions do New Testament writers endorse; is the promised land ultimately relocated in heaven and Earth relegated to the margin of natural history? Does the mission of the church still rely on the imagery of a promised land—a heaven—above? Has the long history of colonial missionaries employing grey texts led to a toleration of those who mistreat new lands and their peoples? Are there texts that justify a mission of the church to the lands themselves—or, indeed, to all creation? Rom 8:18–27 and Col 1:15–20 are green texts that provide principles necessary to guide our reading of all promised land texts or traditions, and move us to hear the cries of a groaning creation.

And if we take the leap of identifying with our groaning planet, the deep dimensions of these texts may move us in new and courageous ways!

> **One group of Australian Indigenous elders, the Rainbow Spirit Elders[13], hears the groaning of creation and the Creator: 'The Creator Spirit is crying because the deep spiritual bonds with the land and its people have been broken. The land is crying because it is slowly dying without this bond of spiritual life. The people are crying because they long for a restoration of that deep spiritual bond with the Creator Spirit and the land.'**

---

13. Rainbow Spirit Elders, *Rainbow Spirit Theology*, 42.

Conclusion

An inconvenient text

The Bible is an inconvenient text for several reasons. First, there are numerous grey texts in which nature is devalued at the hands of God or humans. These texts tend to focus on human interests and suppress the character or voice of Earth or members of the Earth community. These texts are anthropocentric and view nature primarily as a resource for humans to exploit.

Second, the Bible is inconvenient because we are gaining a new eco-consciousness or ecology-informed worldview that tends to make us more empathetic with Earth as the very source of our being and sustenance. We are an integral part of the ecosystem called Earth. As we read with this new consciousness, we are more ready to identify with Earth, read with new eyes and recognise the injustice done to Earth in order to magnify God.

Third, the Bible is also inconvenient because there are a number of texts that can be classified as green. These texts recognise the intrinsic value of Earth, celebrate domains of Earth, remember the sufferings of Earth, or anticipate the revival of Earth as an integral part of a renewed creation.

> **The presence of these green texts highlights the problematic nature of the grey texts, and confronts the reader with the need to choose between grey and green texts as preferred expressions of the voice and mission of the church.**

In the preceding chapters, especially chapter 4, I have explored key dimensions of an emerging cosmology or worldview that is no longer simply informed by our knowledge of space or the theory of evolution, but more specifically, with a consciousness of our identity as organisms that are an integral part of the ecosystems and interdependent life-forces that we call planet Earth. Just as the discovery that Earth is not flat meant re-reading our biblical traditions, the realisation that we are intimately integrated into the Earth ecosystem means, I have argued, that we should no longer remain blind to this reality; rather we should use it to inform our reading of the Bible. The current environmental crisis has hastened the need for and the rise of this new consciousness.

As a result, I have articulated an approach that has three steps; it is based on earlier more complex principles of interpretation. These steps, discussed in chapter 5, involve suspicion, identification and retrieval.

By *suspicion* I mean the awareness that most interpreters in the past and probably most biblical writers themselves have written from an anthropocentric perspective; generally human beings have focused first of all on human interests and relegated creation and the domains of creation to the background.

By *identification* I mean that, given our emerging ecology-informed consciousness, we empathise with Earth and members of the Earth community as we read—rather than only identifying with the human characters of the text. As we identify and empathise with all living beings, we become aware of whether a text is genuinely grey or potentially green.

As we empathise with Earth and the domains of creation, we recognise that these realities are more than mere objects in the text: they are subjects whose role and voice deserve to be heard. *Retrieval* is the process of recovering the voices of Earth and members of the Earth community.

Employing the first of these steps, I identified a selection of texts that are obviously grey. These texts, analysed in chapters 1–3, focus on three categories in the Bible: the mandate to dominate (found especially in Gen 1:26–28); the destructive acts of God (as illustrated in the flood and exodus narratives); and the promised land texts (especially in Deuteronomy and Joshua) where the conquest of a promised land seems to justify violence toward both the people of the land and the land itself.

> **In the Western world these grey texts have been cited at various times to justify actions that have had severe environmental consequences.**

The mandate to dominate has provided the grounds for the so-called harnessing of nature—the destruction of species, the clearing of forests and the exploitation of soils. Emulation of the God who acts violently in history, damaging the domains of creation with accompanying deeds of violence, has led to collateral damage in nature. And colonial powers have used the ideology of the promised land texts to support their conquest of Indigenous peoples and their lands. Some Christian traditions have transposed the concept of the promised land to heaven and relegated Earth to a barren sojourn as a consequence.

In chapters 6–8, I re-read these grey texts and juxtaposed them with green texts in their immediate and wider contexts. By identifying with Earth and specific domains of Earth, I retrieved their voices rising in protest against the destructive attitude of humans and God. I noted that in several of the prophetic books, the prophets themselves hear the land mourning and wild animals crying in anguish.

I also discussed a selection of green texts where humans or God are in a supportive and intimate relationship with Earth or members of the Earth community. In chapter 6, for example, I demonstrated that in Gen 2:15 the first humans are given a mission to 'serve and preserve' Earth. In chapter 7 I explored Psalm 104, a portrait of God immanent in nature and not at work liberating humans by destroying nature. In chapter 8, I considered Leviticus 25–26, which presents the land as God's sanctuary—a place where God walks with people as in Eden rather than as a land to be conquered by holy war.

In addition, I explored some key texts of the New Testament to ascertain whether they are consistent with the grey or the green texts of the Old Testament. In chapter 6, for example, I examined the way of Jesus of Nazareth: Jesus declares that the true path is not to rule like tyrants but to serve just as he does when he gives his life. In chapter 7 I identified the act of God becoming flesh according to John 1 as a radical departure from those grey texts that depict God intervening at the expense of nature. In chapter 8 I recognised the groaning of creation as an integral force in nature: the natural world empathising with the suffering presence of God.

An uncomfortable choice

The preceding analysis has highlighted a radically different orientation between those texts we have designated as grey and those we have found to be green. The outcome of this analysis might be summarised as follows:

a. **Grey texts**: a clear identification of those passages which are grey, promoting an anthropocentric orientation that is at odds with the ecojustice interpreting principles espoused, and destructive for the environment if promoted as mandates or missions for the future.

b. **Green texts:** a recognition of another set of texts that are green, affirming Earth, members of the Earth community and all of creation as having intrinsic value and not merely as resources for human consumption.

c. **Earth voices:** a retrieval of the positive roles and voices of Earth and the Earth community from within the text—a retrieval that reflects an empathy with Earth, an awareness of the emerging ecology-informed worldview, and a willingness to go beyond the dualistic mindset of past interpreters.

The difficulty that I have encountered in promoting a green reading approach is twofold. First, some readers acknowledge the presence of two sets of conflicting passages—the grey and the green—but as yet find it problematic to discern and recognise the voice of Earth as a legitimate voice in the text. And second, despite recognising that these two sets of conflicting passages in the text is inconvenient, the whole Bible nevertheless remains authoritative for many believers.

Accordingly, at the end of chapters 6–8 I have briefly undertaken the task of explaining why we should choose the green texts over the grey texts. For many the need to empathise with Earth and to preserve creation in our current environmental crisis is reason enough to select the green texts and relegate the grey texts to history—just as we have discarded the inconvenient and discredited flat-Earth cosmology of the Old Testament. For others, however, that choice remains more difficult; it represents an uncomfortable choice.

For me the criterion for making a choice is determined not only by my perspective as a human being acutely conscious of my kinship with a suffering Earth, but also by my conviction that the Gospel is the ultimate revelation of God for our suffering creation today. I choose, therefore, as authoritative only those texts that are consistent with the revelation of God in and through Jesus of Nazareth who suffered and died on Calvary.

> **This Gospel principle governs my interpretation of the relevance of the texts in question and their implications for how I relate to creation.**

I will admit that this approach may reflect something of my Lutheran heritage. In terms of my Lutheran tradition, this principle might be summarised in Luther's words as *Was Christum treibet*. I understand this principle as 'What points to Christ'—or, in other words—'What is consistent with the essence of the Gospel: the centre of the Christian Scriptures and the ultimate revelation of God in Christ'. The Gospel revelation supersedes prior revelations; these are now to be read in the light of this revelation. Ultimately, whenever I must make a choice between apparently conflicting revelations, I choose what is consistent with this Gospel principle!

In relation to the three groups of grey and green texts discussed above, the choice of the latter becomes apparent:

> **The mission to serve and guard (Gen 2:15 and parallels) is chosen over the mandate to dominate (Gen 1:26–28 and parallels).**

This choice is clear to me because the way of Jesus of Nazareth is explicitly to 'serve' and not to 'rule', a serving that leads Jesus, the Son of Man, to give his life as a ransom (Mark 10.42-45). The act of God in Christ giving his life as a ransom is the epitome of the Gospel. 'Serving' not 'ruling' is the implication for a life—including our life with creation—lived in accord with this Gospel message.

> **The act of God becoming incarnate in Jesus Christ (John 1:1–14) is chosen as a superior revelation of God's identity over those acts of liberation and judgment (eg, the exodus event) that result in the destruction of various domains of nature.**

Once again, the incarnation of the Word in flesh epitomises the Gospel and means that God becomes one with flesh, a piece of the planet, and is in empathy with all creation. This act of suffering love transcends the acts of violence against creation and forces us to re-read prior portraits of divine revelation.

> **Texts recognising the groaning of creation (Rom 8:17–27) are chosen over those that devalue a given land, Earth, or creation as a whole.**

Texts relating to the groaning of creation here and now because of curses past and present (Rom 8:18–27) are preferable to those that seem to support the conquest of any given land (Joshua) or the devaluing of this creation in favour of a promised land in heaven, or of another creation. The Christ of the Gospel not only reveals the suffering love of God at Calvary, but that God continues to suffer as a cosmic presence in all creation, anticipating its rebirth.

An unenviable task

This is not the place to articulate the ways in which the church or Christians readers ought to undertake a green ministry in the current ecological crisis. There are, it seems to me, a number of tasks we need to undertake if the Bible is to be a viable and integral part of our mission to creation and not simply a source of isolated green texts. These tasks involve a serious re-orientation of our thinking in line with the analysis and choice of texts discussed above.

Our first task is to
- **listen** with empathy to the cries of nature suffering from centuries of abuse at the hands of humanity;
- **liberate** ourselves from the mandate to dominate and other grey texts that support our assumed superiority over nature;
- **learn** anew the art of serving Earth as our mother, relating to nature as our kin and being guardians of our planet home.

Our second task is to
- **listen** with empathy to the cries of injustice rising from domains of nature destroyed by God to punish or liberate humans in grey texts of the Bible;
- **liberate** ourselves from being dominated by a tradition of grey texts that depicts God's mighty acts as frequently resulting in collateral damage to nature;
- **learn** to discern and celebrate the presence of our God incarnate deep in the ecosystems that permeate our planet.

Our third task is to
- **listen** with empathy to the cries of so-called promised lands and their peoples who experienced devaluation and destruction at the hands of invaders who claim God's mandate for their holy war of destructive conquest;

- **liberate** ourselves from the orientation of grey texts and traditions that devalue Earth—whether as land to be conquered or a domain to be abandoned in favour of a promised land above;
- **learn** that our hearing the groanings of creation and the Spirit is an integral part of our mission to heal this planet sanctuary called Earth.

> **Our unenviable task, then, is liberate ourselves from the power of those grey texts that have controlled our thinking; and through green texts to listen with empathy to cries of a suffering creation, and discern God's presence in solidarity with all who suffer.**

A final challenge

I would like to close with a final challenge—a green text that has been relegated to the margin by most interpreters: Mark 16:15.

> And he (Jesus) said to them, 'Go into all the world and proclaim the good news to the whole creation.'
> (Mark 16:15)

Now I can immediately hear some scholars screaming that this text is probably not part of the original manuscript of the Gospel of Mark.

True! So we do not know who wrote it! But then, neither do we know who wrote the letter to the Hebrews. This text may not have been written by Mark, but added to Mark; many scholars would argue that some of the epistles were not written by St Paul, but they have been included and added to his corpus of letters. My point is that very early in the Christian era, a person or a community believed that this ending was important, reflected Jesus' message and was consistent with the Gospel of Mark.

The mission of the Christian church has focused almost exclusively on the commission of Jesus in Matt 28:19 enjoining the disciples to proclaim the good news to all nations. And given this context, the commission in Mark has understandably been read in the light of the Matthew text and therefore interpreted to mean that proclaiming the Gospel to 'all creation' refers to preaching to 'all humans'.

The Greek term (*ktisis*) in the Mark passage, however, refers to the whole physical creation, not simply to human beings. Whether or not Mark wrote these specific words, there was apparently an early tradition that Jesus enjoined proclaiming the good news to all creation: Earth, ocean, atmosphere—and beyond.

Our final challenge is this: what precisely is this good news for the whole of creation—for the fauna, the flora, the mountains, the waters, and the mines? In the light of my analysis in the preceding chapters, I suggest the following would indeed be good news for creation to hear.

❖ A message for Earth and the Earth community that *the mandate to dominate has been revoked by God in Christ*—or put another way: the mandate to dominate has been superseded by a commission of Christ to serve and sustain creation!

❖ An assurance addressed to creation that *God in Christ will no longer violate nature to liberate humans*; with the incarnation of God in Christ, the mighty acts of God involve a divine empathy that leads to the healing of nature—rather than an indifference that tolerates unjust deeds of destruction toward nature.

❖ A message to planet Earth that *God empathises with the groaning of creation* and summons Christians to do the same—in anticipation of healed creation rather than the dream of a promised land in heaven or in the distant future.

In order to share the message we are called to proclaim to creation, we first need to undertake the unenviable task of liberating ourselves from the mandate to dominate, those grey texts that portray our God as violent toward nature and dreams that devalue Earth as transient. It is time for us to empathise with our Earth and our kin in Earth community, and to celebrate and enact the blessing and healing our God gives exuberantly to all creation.

Bibliography

Allaby, Michael. *A Dictionary of Ecology* (2nd edition; Oxford: Oxford University Press, 1998).

Balabanski, Vicky. 'John 1—The Earth Bible Challenge: An Intra-textual Approach to Reading John 1', in Norman Habel & Vicky Balabanski (eds), *The Earth Story in the New Testament* (The Earth Bible 5; Sheffield: Sheffield Academic Press, 2002): 89–94.

———'Critiquing Anthroprocentric Cosmology: Retrieving Stoic "Permeation Cosmology" in Colossians 1.15–20', in Norman Habel and Peter Trudinger (eds), *Exploring Ecological Hermeneutics* (Atlanta: SBL, 2008): 151–160.

Barrett, Grahame, Paul Payten & Steve Goldsmith. *Your Eco Handbook. Achieving a Sustainable Future* (Sydney: Fairfax Books, 2007).

Berry, Thomas & Brian Swimme. *The Universe Story* (New York: HarperSan Francisco, 1992).

Berry, Thomas. *The Great Work. Our Way into the Future* (New York: Bell Tower, 1999).

Boston, Jonathan. 'Tackling Global Warming—Now or Never', in *Tui Motu InterIslands* 55, June 2008: 13–15.

Brueggemann, Walter. *The Land* (Philadelphia: Fortress Press, 2002).

Byrne, Brendan. 'Creation Groaning: an Earth Bible Reading of Romans 8.18–22', in Norman Habel & Shirley Wurst (eds), *Readings from the Perspective of Earth* (The Earth Bible 1; Sheffield: Sheffield Academic Press, 2000): 193–208.

Cadwallader, Alan. '"And the Earth Shook"—Mortality and Ecological Diversity: Interpreting Jesus' Death in Matthew's Gospel', in Denis Edwards & Mark Worthing (eds), *Biodiversity and Ecology: An Interdisciplinary Challenge* (Adelaide: ATF Press, 2004): 45–54.

———*Beyond the Word of Woman. Recovering the Bodies of Syrophoenician Women* (Adelaide: ATF Press, 2008).

Carley, Keith. 'An Apology for Domination', in Norman Habel & Shirley Wurst (eds), *Readings from the Perspective of Earth* (The Earth Bible 1; Sheffield: Sheffield Academic Press, 2000): 111–24.

Clements, Janice. *Arno Bay and District 1883–1983* (Arno Bay Centenary Committee, 1982).

Darragh, Neil. *At Home in the Earth* (Auckland: Accent Publications, 2000).

Eaton, Heather. 'Ecological-Feminist Theology: Contributions and Challenges', in Dieter Hessel (ed), *Theology for Earth Community: a Field Guide* (Maryknoll: Orbis, 1996): 77–92.

———'Ecofeminist Contributions to an Ecojustice Hermeneutic', in Norman Habel & Shirley Wurst (eds), *Readings from the Perspective of Earth* (The Earth Bible 1; Sheffield: Sheffield Academic Press, 2000): 54–71.

Edwards, Denis. *Ecology at the Heart of Faith; The Change of Heart that Leads to a New Way of Living on Earth* (New York: Orbis, 2006).

Fergusson, David. *The Cosmos and the Creator. An Introduction to the Theology of Creation* (London: SPCK, 1998).

Fretheim, Terence. 'The Reclamation of Creation: Redemption and Law in Exodus', *Interpretation* 45, 1991: 354–65.

Galambush, Julie. 'Castles in the Air: Creation as Property in Ezekiel', in *Ezekiel's Hierarchical World—Wrestling with Tiered Reality* (Symposium 31; Atlanta: SBL, 2004): 91–108.

Gardner, Anne. 'Ecojustice: a Study of Genesis 6.11–13', in Norman Habel & Shirley Wurst (eds), *The Earth Story in Genesis* (The Earth Bible 2; Sheffield: Sheffield Academic Press, 2000): 117–29.

Garr, W Randall. *In His Own Image and Likeness. Humanity, Divinity, and Monotheism* (Leiden: Brill, 2003).

Goodenough, Ursula. *The Sacred Depths of Nature* (Oxford: Oxford University Press, 1998).

Habel, Norman. The Two Flood Stories in Genesis', in Alan Dundes (ed), *The Flood Myth* (Berkeley: University of California Press, 1988): 13–18.

———*The Land Is Mine. Six Biblical Land Ideologies* (Minneaopolis: Fortress, 1995).

———'Geophany: the Earth Story in Genesis One', in Norman Habel & Shirley Wurst (eds), *The Earth Story in Genesis* (The Earth Bible 2; Sheffield: Sheffield Academic Press, 2000), 34–48.

———'Ecojustice Challenge: Is Earth Valued in John 1', in Norman Habel & Vicky Balabanski (eds), *The Earth Story in the New Testament* (The Earth Bible 5; Sheffield: Sheffield Academic Press, 2002): 76–82.

———'The Implications of God Discovering Wisdom in Earth', in Ellen van Wolde (ed), *Job 28: Cognition in Context* (Leiden: Brill, 2003): 281–98.

——— 'The Silence of the Lands: The Ecojustice Implications of Ezekiel's Judgement Oracles', in *Ezekiel's Hierarchical World—Wrestling with Tiered Reality* (Symposium 31; Atlanta: SBL, 2004): 127–40.

——— 'What Kind of God would Destroy Earth Anyway? An Ecojustice Reading of the Flood Narrative', in Wesley Bergen & Emin Siedlecki (eds), *Voyages in Unchartered Waters. Essays in the Theory and Practice of Biblical Interpretation* (Sheffield: Sheffield Phoenix Press, 2006a): 203–11.

——— 'Playing God or Playing Earth? An Ecological Reading of Genesis 1.26–28', in *And God Saw that It Was Good: Essays on Creation and God in Honor of Terence E. Fretheim.* (Word and World Supplement Series 5; St Paul: Luther Seminary, 2006b): 33–41.

———'Introducing Ecological Hermeneutics', in Norman Habel & Peter Trudinger (eds), *Exploring Ecological Hermeneutics* (SBL Symposium; Atlanta: SBL, 2008) 1–8.

Habel, Norman (ed). *Reading the Bible from the Perspective of Earth* (The Earth Bible 1; Sheffield: Sheffield Academic Press, 2000).

Habel, Norman & Shirley Wurst (eds). *The Earth Story in Genesis One* (The Earth Bible 2; Sheffield: Sheffield Academic Press, 2000).

Harris, Michael. *One Blood: 200 Years of Aboriginal Encounter with Christianity; a Story of Hope* (Sydney: Albatross Books, 1990).

Hiebert, Theodore. 'Re-imaging Nature: Shifts in Biblical Interpretation', *Interpretation* 50, 1995: 36–46.

Hillel, Daniel. *The Natural History of the Bible. An Environmental Exploration of the Hebrew Scriptures* (New York: Columbia University Press, 2006).

Hort, Greta. 'The Plagues of Egypt', *Zeitscrfit fur alttestamentliche Wissenschaft* 69, 1957: 85–103; 70, 1958: 48–59.

Jennings, William H. *Storms over Genesis. Biblical Battleground in America's Wars of Religion* (Minneapolis: AugsburgFortress, 2007).

Kaessmann, Margot. 'Covenant, Praise and Justice in Creation. Five Bible Studies', in David Hallman (ed), *Ecotheology: Voices from South and North* (Maryknoll: Orbis, 1994): 28–51.

Lemche, Niels Peter. *The Canaanites and Their Land. The Tradition of the*

Canaanites (JSOT Supplement Series 110; Sheffield: Journal for the Study of the Old Testament Press, 1991).

Limburg, James. 'Who Cares for the Earth? Psalm Eight and the Environment', in AJ Hultgren et al (eds), *All Things New* (Word and World Supplement Series 1; St Paul: Lutheran Theological Seminary, 1991): 43–52.

Lovelock, James. *The Revenge of Gaia* (London: Allen Lane, 2006).

Macy, Joanna & John Seed, 'Gaia Meditations', in Roger S Gottlieb (ed), *This Sacred Earth: Religion, Nature, Environment* (New York: Routledge, 1996), 501.

Marcus, J. *Mark 1–8: a New Translation with Introduction and Commentary* (Anchor Bible 27; New York: Doubleday, 2000).

Marlow,Hilary. 'The Other Prophet! The Voice of Earth in the Book of Amos', in Norman Habel & Peter Trudinger (eds), *Exploring Ecological Hermeneutics* (SBL Symposium; Atlanta: SBL, 2008): 75–84.

McBride, S. Dean. 'Divine Protocol: Genesis 1.1–2.3 as Prologue to the Pentateuch', in William Brown & S Dean McBride (eds), *God Who Creates* (Grand Rapids: Eerdmanns, 2000): 3–41.

McDonagh, Sean. *To Care for the Earth. A Call to a New Theology* (London: Geoffrey Chapman, 1986).

McFague, Sallie. *A New Climate for Theology. God, the World and Global Warming* (Minneapolis: Fortress, 2008).

Miller, Patrick. *Genesis 1–11: Studies in Structure and Theme* (Journal for the Study of the Old Testament Supplement Series 8; Sheffield: Sheffield Academic Press, 1978).

Miller, Susan. 'The Descent of Darkness over the Land. Listening to the Voice of Earth in Mark 14.3–9', in Norman Habel &Peter Trudinger (eds), *Exploring Ecological Hermeneutics* (SBL Symposium; Atlanta: SBL, 2008): 123–30.

Nash, James. *Loving Nature: Ecological Integrity and Christian Responsibility* (Nashville: Abingdon, 1991).

Orlinsky, Harry. 'The Biblical Concept of the Land of Israel: Cornerstone of the Covenant between God and Israel', in LA Hoffman (ed), *The Land of Israel: Jewish Perspectives* (Notre Dame: University of Notre Dame Press, 19861986): 27–64.

Palmer, Clare. 'Stewardship: A Case Study in Environmental Ethics', in Ian Ball et al (eds), *The Earth Beneath: a Critical Guide to Green Theology* (London: SPCK, 1992): 67–86.

Polkinghorne, John. *The Faith of a Physicist: Reflections of a Bottom-up Thinker* (Minneapolis: AugsburgFortress, 1995).

Provan, Iain. *Tenants in God's Land. Earth-keeping and People-keeping in the Old Testament* (Cambridge: Grove Books, 2008).

Prior, Michael. *The Bible and Colonialism: a Moral Critique* (Sheffield: Sheffield Academic Press, 1997).

Raheb, Mitri. 'Land, People and Identities: a Palestinian Perspective' (*2006 Charles Strong Trust Lecture;* see www.charlesstrongtrust.org. au/ lectures).

Rainbow Spirit Elders. *Rainbow Spirit Theology. Towards an Australian Aboriginal Theology* (2nd edn; Hindmarsh, South Australia: ATF Press, 2007).

Robb, Carol S. 'Introduction', in Carol Robb & CJ Casebolt (eds), *Covenant for a New Creation: Ethics, Religion and Public Policy* (Maryknoll: Orbis, 1991): 1–23.

Rossing, Barbara. 'Alas for Earth! Lament and Resistance in Revelation 12', in Norman Habel & Vicky Balabanski (eds), *The Earth Story in the New Testament* (The Earth Bible 5; Sheffield: Sheffield Academic Press, 2002): 180–92.

———'Hastening the Day when the Earth Will Burn? Global Warming, Revelation and 2 Peter 3', in *Currents in Theology and Mission* 35, 2008: 361–71.

Ruether, Rosemary. *God and Gaia: an Ecofeminist Theology of Earth Healing* (San Francisco: Harper, 1992).

Santmire, H. Paul. *Nature Reborn: the Ecological and Cosmic Promise of Christian Theology* (Minneapolis: AugsburgFortress, 2000).

Soelle, Dorothea. *Of War and Love* (Maryknoll, New York: Orbis, 1981).

Suzuki, David & Kathy Vanderlinden. *You Are the Earth* (Sydney, NSW: Allen & Unwin, 1999).

Swartz, Daniel. 'Jews, Jewish Texts and Nature: a Brief History', in Roger Gottlieb (ed), *This Sacred Earth. Religion, Nature and the Environment* (New York: Routledge, 1995): 87–103.

Tonstad, Sigve. 'Creation Groaning in Labour Pains', in Norman Habel & Peter Trudinger (eds), *Exploring Ecological Hermeneutics* (SBL Symposium; Atlanta: SBL, 2008): 141–50.

Towner, Sibley. 'The Future of Nature', in *Interpretation* 50 (1996): 27–35.

Tubbs Loya, Melissa. '"Therefore the Earth Mourns": The Grievance of the Land in Hosea 4.1–3', in Norman Habel & Peter Trudinger, eds. *Exploring Ecological Hermeneutics* (SBL Symposium; Atlanta: SBL, 2008): 53–62.

Von Rad, Gerhard. *Genesis. A Commentary* (Philadelphia: Westminster, 1961).

Wainwright, Elaine. 'Which Intertext? A Response to an Ecojustice Challenge: Is Earth Valued in John 1?', in Norman Habel & Vicky Balabanski (eds), *The Earth Story in the New Testament* (The Earth Bible 5; Sheffield: Sheffield Academic Press, 2002): 76–82.

Westermann, Claus. *The Genesis Accounts of Creation* (Philadelphia: Fortress, 1964).

White, Lynn Jr. 'The Historical Roots of Our Ecological Crisis', *Science* 155, 1967: 1203–7.

Wurst, Shirley. 'Beloved Come Back to Me: Ground's Theme Song in Genesis 3', in Norman Habel & Shirley Wurst (eds), *The Earth Story in Genesis* (The Earth Bible 2; Sheffield: Sheffield Academic Press, 2000), 87–104.

Subject Index

Biblical Index